MW01206432

Language Minority Students with Disabilities

Leonard M. Baca
Estella Almanza

 Published by The Council for Exceptional Children

 A Product of the ERIC Clearinghouse
on Handicapped and Gifted Children

Library of Congress Catalog Card Number 91-58309

ISBN 0-86586-214-1

A product of the ERIC / OSEP Special Project, the ERIC Clearinghouse on Handicapped and Gifted Children

Published in 1991 by The Council for Exceptional Children, 1920 Association Drive, Reston, Virginia 22091-1589
Stock No. P357

This publication was prepared with funding from the U.S. Department of Education, Office of Special Education Programs, contract no. RI88062007. Contractors undertaking such projects under government sponsorship are encouraged to express freely their judgment in professional and technical matters. Prior to publication the manuscript was submitted for critical review and determination of professional competence. This publication has met such standards. Points of view, however, do not necessarily represent the official view or opinions of either The Council for Exceptional Children or the Department of Education.

Printed in the United States of America
10 9 8 7 6 5 4 3 2

Contents

Foreword

EXCEPTIONAL CHILDREN AT RISK
CEC Mini-Library

Many of today's pressing social problems, such as poverty, homelessness, drug abuse, and child abuse, are factors that place children and youth at risk in a variety of ways. There is a growing need for special educators to understand the risk factors that students must face and, in particular, the risks confronting children and youth who have been identified as exceptional. A child may be at risk *due to* a number of quite different phenomena, such as poverty or abuse. Therefore, the child may be at risk *for* a variety of problems, such as developmental delays; debilitating physical illnesses or psychological disorders; failing or dropping out of school; being incarcerated; or generally having an unrewarding, unproductive adulthood. Compounding the difficulties that both the child and the educator face in dealing with these risk factors is the unhappy truth that a child may have more than one risk factor, thereby multiplying his or her risk and need.

The struggle within special education to address these issues was the genesis of the 1991 CEC conference "Children on the Edge." The content for the conference strands is represented by this series of publications, which were developed through the assistance of the Division of Innovation and Development of the U.S. Office of Special Education Programs (OSEP). OSEP funds the ERIC/OSEP Special Project, a research dissemination activity of The Council for Exceptional Children. As a part of its publication program, which synthesizes and translates research in special education for a variety of audiences, the ERIC/OSEP Special Project coordinated the development of this series of books and assisted in their dissemination to special education practitioners.

Each book in the series pertains to one of the conference strands. Each provides a synthesis of the literature in its area, followed by practical suggestions—derived from the literature—for program developers, administrators, and teachers. The 11 books in the series are as follows:

- *Programming for Aggressive and Violent Students* addresses issues that educators and other professionals face in contending with episodes of violence and aggression in the schools.

- *Abuse and Neglect of Exceptional Children* examines the role of the special educator in dealing with children who are abused and neglected and those with suspected abuse and neglect.

- *Special Health Care in the School* provides a broad-based definition of the population of students with special health needs and discusses their unique educational needs.

- *Homeless and in Need of Special Education* examines the plight of the fastest growing segment of the homeless population, families with children.

- *Hidden Youth: Dropouts from Special Education* addresses the difficulties of comparing and drawing meaning from dropout data prepared by different agencies and examines the characteristics of students and schools that place students at risk for leaving school prematurely.

- *Born Substance Exposed, Educationally Vulnerable* examines what is known about the long-term effects of exposure *in utero* to alcohol and other drugs, as well as the educational implications of those effects.

- *Depression and Suicide: Special Education Students at Risk* reviews the role of school personnel in detecting signs of depression and potential suicide and in taking appropriate action, as well as the role of the school in developing and implementing treatment programs for this population.

- *Language Minority Students with Disabilities* discusses the preparation needed by schools and school personnel to meet the needs of limited-English-proficient students with disabilities.

- *Alcohol and Other Drugs: Use, Abuse, and Disabilities* addresses the issues involved in working with children and adolescents who have disabling conditions and use alcohol and other drugs.

- *Rural, Exceptional, At Risk* examines the unique difficulties of delivering education services to at-risk children and youth with exceptionalities who live in rural areas.

- *Double Jeopardy: Pregnant and Parenting Youth in Special Education* addresses the plight of pregnant teenagers and teenage parents, especially those in special education, and the role of program developers and practitioners in responding to their educational needs.

Background information applicable to the conference strand on juvenile corrections can be found in another publication, *Special Education in Juvenile Corrections*, which is a part of the CEC Mini-Library *Working with Behavioral Disorders*. That publication addresses the demographics of incarcerated youth and promising practices in responding to their needs.

1. Introduction

Limited English proficient (LEP) students with disabilities are often at risk because schools are not sufficiently prepared to meet their needs. The native languages and cultures of these students should be considered strengths upon which to build an appropriate education.

Rationale

Given the current demographic realities, students with limited English proficiency (LEP)—or students who are potentially English proficient (PEP), as suggested by Hamayan (1990)—will continue to increase in numbers more rapidly than other student groups. These students are often at risk for not realizing their full potential because they tend to underachieve in mainstream classes. In many cases they are inappropriately identified as having disabilities when they do not (Carrasquillo, 1991; Hamayan & Damico, 1991). Even when these students are *properly* identified as having disabilities, often they are not provided with appropriate bilingual, multicultural, or English-as-a-second-language (ESL) services within the context of their individualized educational program (IEPs) and special education placements (Baca, 1990). These students' language and/or cultural differences are often mistaken as characteristics of disabling conditions. Their language and cultural strengths, as well as needs, are not integrated into their special education services.

Students with limited English proficiency need high-quality native language instruction and/or ESL services within the context of special education in order to reach their full academic potential. Both regular and special education teachers will need additional training to work effectively with these students.

Assumptions

The first critical assumption or premise operating throughout this book is that language and cultural differences can and should be considered strengths. The language and culture of these students should be viewed as part of the *solution* rather than as part of the problem. These differences are not deficits, and they should not be considered disabling conditions. A second important assumption of this paper is that limited English proficiency is not a barrier to school success unless the school and its staff are not proficient in bilingual/multicultural and ESL regular and special education. The final assumption is that the educational environment of students with limited English proficiency places them progressively more at risk when the school is unable to respond appropriately to their needs without fragmenting services. These students are even further at risk when poverty and issues of race and color are part of their background. In other words, for students with limited English proficiency, the danger is cumulative.

2. Synthesis of Research

The educational needs of language minority students with disabilities are a new area of research. Nonetheless, there are a number of scholars doing work in this emerging field. A synthesis of the findings is reported under the categories of prereferral, assessment, and instruction.

Student Needs

Students from language minority groups can be gifted, of average ability, or have disabilities. If schools are able to provide appropriate services for them, they will not be at risk. However, if they have limited English proficiency and attend schools that are limited in their ability to offer native language instruction and high-quality ESL instruction, they will certainly be at risk of failing to thrive and develop their full potential. Students with limited English proficiency who also have disabilities, according to special education criteria, are almost always at risk in U.S. schools today. This group of students is generally referred to in the bilingual/multicultural special education literature as *culturally and linguistically different exceptional (CLDE)* students (Baca, 1990; Carrasquillo & Baecher, 1991).

Although the exact number is not known, it has been estimated that there are approximately 1 million students in the United States who have limited English proficiency and who also have serious learning and/or behavior disorders and needs that may qualify them for special education services (Baca & Cervantes, 1989). These CLDE students have been referred to in the literature as *triple threat students* (Rueda & Chan, 1979). Many of them have three strikes against them before they even get an opportunity to step into the batter's box (school). The first strike is a behavior and/or learning disability; the second is the limited English proficiency; and the third is poverty and all the concomitant limitations it imposes on the educational experience. It has also been suggested that the factors of race and ethnicity be added to this list. When these students are Hispanic, Asian, or American Indian along with being poor, having limited English proficiency, and having disabilities, they are at extreme risk.

The CLDE student population has never been targeted as a specific population in need of legislation, categorical support, and specialized services. For this and other reasons, these students usually fall between the cracks of special categorical programs such as bilingual education, special education, and Chapter I services, and thus they remain for the most part underserved and inappropriately served.

There are currently approximately 5 million students with disabilities in U.S. public schools. The large majority of these students fall into the mildly and moderately disabled categories and approximately 90% are in socially constructed categories such as learning disabilities, emotional disturbance/behavior disorders, mild and moderate mental retardation, and speech and communication disorders.

The distinction between socially constructed categories such as learning disabilities and emotional disturbance and physical/organic categories such as deaf and blind is an important one. Socially constructed categories are to a great extent a consequence of social and professional norms and thus subject to change over time and across various cultural and national groups. It has also been suggested that inadequate schools and inappropriate instruction or schooling may be responsible for creating disabling conditions for students (Cummins, 1989; Mehen, Hertweck, & Meihls, 1986). For this reason, it is important to include a discussion about a larger group of students who do not necessarily have disabilities but are likely to be identified as having disabilities as they progress through school. This group is generally referred to as the *high risk population*—students who have been described as having many of the characteristics of students in the socially constructed categories. As a group, they achieve below grade level and leave school before graduation in disproportionate numbers.

According to Fradd and Correa (1989), *high risk* refers to students who are physically, medically, and psychologically in danger of failing to thrive. Also included are students who do not speak English as their first language and whose educational opportunities are limited because of their lower socioeconomic status and cultural differences based on race and/or ethnicity. Perhaps the greatest risk factor some of these students face is that their schools, curricula, and teachers are disadvantaged in the sense that they are not able to communicate with them in their native language or understand their culture, motivational patterns, and academic learning styles. This points to the need for improved teacher training programs as well as more appropriate curricula and materials for the at-risk as well as the CLDE student population.

Both high-risk and CLDE students can benefit from instruction in their stronger and more proficient language. In many cases this is the native language. Fradd and Vega (1987) have indicated that use of a student's non-English language is a central issue when the student has both limited English proficiency and a disability. Bernal (1974) appears to have been the first educator to have advocated in print for a bilingual instructional program for CLDE students. Baca and Cervantes (1989) and Ortiz and Yates (1983) have also recommended the use of a bilingual instructional approach for CLDE students.

Bilingual/Multicultural Special Education Defined

The term *bilingual* generally means the ability to use two languages. Since the degree of proficiency in the two languages can vary considerably, Hornby (1977) suggested that it is not an all-or-none property, but an individual characteristic that may exist to varying degrees from minimal ability to complete fluency in more than one language. A broad definition of bilingual/multicultural education that is widely accepted is *the use of two languages and cultures as media of instruction.* The primary purpose of bilingual education, according to the consensus of experts, is to improve cognitive and affective development (Blanco, 1977). In other words, the primary goal of bilingual education is not to teach English or a second language but to teach children academic and social skills through the language and cultural perspective they know best and to reinforce this in the second language, English.

Special Education is generally defined as an individually designed program of instruction implemented by a specialist for a student whose learning and/or behavior needs cannot be adequately met in the regular program of instruction. Bilingual/multicultural special education is defined, for the purposes of this book, as *the use of the home language and the home culture along with English in an individually designed program of special instruction for the student.* In other words, bilingual/multicultural special education considers the student's native language and culture as strengths and important resources that provide the foundation for an appropriate and effective education.

The ultimate goal of bilingual/multicultural special education is to help the CLDE student reach his or her maximum potential for learning. Although teaching English as well as the native language is important, it should not become the primary purpose. Making it the primary purpose would cause a classic means-end inversion that could prove harmful to the student. For example, if a special educator or a bilingual special educator considered the CLDE student's primary need to be the acquisition of English, valuable instructional time for teaching concepts and academic skills would be lost. Thus, the focus should be on how to teach concepts and academic skills through an ESL approach as well as through the native language whenever possible.

Evaluation and Research

Early research in this new field was conducted by scholars in regular education, special education, and bilingual education, along with researchers from anthropology, psychology, linguistics, and sociology. They began by extrapolating and applying the theoretical principles and research findings from these areas to CLDE students. The information gathered became the building blocks for designing services and programs for this unique population of learners. For example, one of the classic studies quoted in the early bilingual/multicultural special education literature is taken from the bilingual education work of Malherbe (1969), who reported that the children involved in the bilingual schools in South Africa performed significantly better in language attainment (in both languages), geography, and arithmetic, than comparable monolingual children. This study was considered significant to the CLDE population because it was one of the few studies up to that time that had controlled for intelligence. In his report, Malherbe stated:

> There is a theory that while the clever child may survive the use of the second language as a medium, the duller child suffers badly. We therefore made the comparison at different intelligence levels and found that not only the bright children but also the children with below normal intelligence do better school work all around in the bilingual school than in the unilingual school. What is most significant is that the greatest gain for the bilingual school was registered in the second language by the lower intelligence groups. (p. 78)

In a related investigation by Buddenhagen in 1971 (cited by McLaughlin, 1984), initial language acquisition at the age of 18 was reported for a student with severe mental retardation who was mute and who was diagnosed as having Down syndrome. This case was similar to the feral child syndrome described in *The Wild Boy of Aveyron* (Itard, 1962).

Baca and Bransford (1982) summarized the findings of five program evaluation studies that reported significant gains on the part of CLDE students in bilingual/multicultural special education programs. The major results of these studies were as follows:

1. Spanish-speaking students with disabilities in New York made significant reading gains (Lesser, 1975).

2. This Title VII program in New York reported that a combined bilingual and special education resource room was meeting the needs of bilingual special education students with significant results (Project Build, 1980).

3. Significant language and learning gains were reported for 3- to 5-year-old CLDE students in a bilingual handicapped children's early education program (HCEEP) operating in the state of Colorado (Weiss, 1980).

4. Statistically significant gains were reported for Spanish-speaking migrant students in a bilingual oral language program among students of both high and low ability (McConnell, 1981).

5. Eighteen programs throughout the central United States demonstrated initial success in educating bilingual students with disabilities (Evans, 1980).

The Office of Bilingual Education and Minority Languages Affairs (OBEMLA) sponsored a study of mainstreamed LEP students with disabilities in elementary school bilingual education programs (Vasquez Nuttall, Goldman, & Landurand, 1983). They described the purpose of this study as an attempt to determine how bilingual educators were coping with these children. This descriptive study of 21 local school districts from all regions of the United States focused on three areas. The first was identification, assessment, and placement; the second was instruction of mainstreamed LEP students in bilingual classrooms; and the third was inservice training for staff serving these students. The major results they reported were as follows:

1. LEP students with disabilities were identified and placed in bilingual special education programs via the IEP process when there were bilingual special education services available to them (33% of the time in this study).

2. When bilingual special education services were not available, students tended not to be identified as having disabilities and remained the responsibility of regular bilingual education.

3. For non-Hispanic LEP students with disabilities, bilingual special education programs were rare, and these students tended to receive ESL rather than native language instruction.

4. Most districts reported that they did not refer LEP students to special education without first modifying their regular bilingual instructional program.

5. The testing approaches used most were the common culture, non-verbal, and test translations. Only a third of the districts reported using the newer, less biased, multipluralistic approaches.

6. Most of the local education agencies (LEAs) allowed LEP students with disabilities to stay in bilingual programs longer than LEP students without disabilities—up to 5 years in three of the districts.

7. LEP students who may have had disabilities but who had not been placed in special education were monitored by the bilingual program utilizing bilingual education criteria.

8. Bilingual teachers used regular bilingual curricula and materials with LEP students with disabilities.

9. Most bilingual teachers reported that they adapted their instruction for LEP students with disabilities by simplifying instructions, providing more repetition, and designing worksheets with larger print and fewer words.

10. None of the bilingual directors gave evidence of having focused specifically on the curricular needs of LEP students with disabilities.

11. Inservice training was greatly needed for both special education teachers and bilingual teachers to be able to understand and work with LEP students with disabilities.

12. The best bilingual special education programs and leadership were developed through the bilingual program.

13. Most LEAs had not found effective ways of training LEP parents to become involved in the education of their children with disabilities.

14. There was a shortage of bilingual special education instructional and ancillary personnel.

15. It appeared that there was underrepresentation of LEP students in special education for 13 of the 21 districts studied.

In the early 1980s the Office of Special Education and Rehabilitative Services (OSERS) sponsored two Handicapped Minority Research Institutes in California and Texas. Although the California institute lost its funding early in the contract period, the research conducted through these two projects represents the first formal and systematic research agenda related to bilingual special education. This research was carried out by the University of Texas at Austin under the leadership of Alba Ortiz and by the Southwest Educational Laboratory in Los Angeles under the direction of Robert Rueda. A synthesis of this information was compiled by Figueroa (1989) and is summarized in Figure 1.

Since the OSERS research, Rueda (1984) and Goldman and Rueda (1988) have reported positive outcomes related to metalinguistic awareness and writing skill development for bilingual children with exceptionalities. In the latter study, Goldman and Rueda concluded that

FIGURE 1
Summary of Findings from the Texas and California
Handicapped Minority Research Institutes

Assessment

1. Language proficiency is not taken into account seriously in special education assessment.
2. Testing is done primarily in English.
3. Problems with a second language are misinterpreted as disabilities.
4. Learning disabilities and communication disorders placements have replaced the misplacement of children in programs for students with educable mental retardation of the 1960s and 1970s.
5. Psychometric test scores from Spanish or English tests are capricious, although paradoxically internally sound.
6. Special education placement leads to decreased test scores.
7. Home data are not used in assessment.
8. The same few tests are used with most children, and they are no different from those used with students from nonminority backgrounds.

Instruction

1. The behaviors that trigger teacher referral suggest that English language acquisition stages and the interaction with English-only programs are being confused for disabling conditions.
2. Few children receive support in their primary language before special education, even fewer during special education.
3. The second and third grades are critical for students with limited English proficiency in terms of potentially being referred.
4. Prereferral modifications of regular programs are rare and give little indication of support in the primary language.
5. Special education produces little academic development.
6. The few special education classes that do work for bilingual students resemble good regular bilingual education classes (whole-language emphasis, comprehensive input, cooperative learning, student empowerment) more than they resemble traditional behavioristic, task-analysis driven, worksheet-oriented special education classes.

Note. Summarized from Figueroa (1989).

it is likely that a critical feature of writing instruction for these students is the establishment of an interactional context that can provide the appropriate scaffolding for them to advance. They argued that bilingual children with exceptionalities should be allowed to bring their own materials and native languages into the classroom.

Another recent study by Harris, Rueda, and Supancheck (1990) described literacy events in special education in three linguistically diverse high schools in Southern California. The findings, gathered from 15 classrooms, indicated the following: English was the preferred language of instruction and print materials; instruction occurred primarily within two interactional structures (i.e., teacher and student and student working alone with no peer interaction); and interaction was dominated by the teacher and involved the traditional initiate-respond-evaluate cycle with no student-initiated interaction reported.

Prereferral Intervention

Prereferral intervention should be considered the cornerstone of bilingual/multicultural special education. It should occur in both monolingual and bilingual regular classroom settings. The term *prereferral* refers to the time period following an indication by a teacher or a concerned person that the student has some kind of learning or behavior problem, but before a formal referral for special education occurs (Baca, Collier, Jacobs, & Hill, 1991). Although the term is widely used in the literature, it is a poor one because it suggests that special education placement is imminent. Graden (1989) explained that prereferral intervention is intended to develop a support system that provides assistance to students in general education classrooms. Therefore, prereferral intervention should be conceptualized as "intervention assistance" emphasizing problem solving (p. 228). Pugach and Johnson (1989) stated that it might be better to conceptualize prereferral intervention as the daily responsibility of classroom teachers. It is of utmost importance that prereferral intervention not be considered a process leading to special education placement, but rather a routine delivery of academic intervention by all educators in order to meet diverse student needs outside of special education.

Prereferral intervention is generally divided into two types: school-based problem-solving teams and consultation by special education teachers (Pugach & Johnson, 1989). Prereferral committees have different titles in different parts of the country, and various prereferral intervention committee models propose different membership. Two distinct examples are Child Study Teams (CSTs) and Teacher Assistance Teams (TATs). CSTs include psychologists, special education teachers, nurses, counselors, and administrators. TATs (Chalfant & Pysh, 1981;

Chalfant, Pysh, Moultrie, 1979) are made up of regular classroom teachers (Ortiz, 1990b).

According to Pugach and Johnson (1989), CSTs should operate under the auspices of regular education and should include bilingual and ESL personnel. If a special educator or a speech and language specialist is involved, it should be as a consultant to the team of regular classroom personnel. Special education staff should be viewed only as contributors to prereferral efforts (Pugach & Johnson, 1989). Accommodating individual differences to promote student academic success is primarily the responsibility of classroom teachers (Ortiz & Maldonado-Colon, 1986). The basic and most essential element of prereferral intervention is the implementation of alternative curricula and instructional interventions and/or behavioral management approaches within the regular monolingual or bilingual instructional setting. When the intervention occurs under the official auspices of special education, it can no longer be considered a prereferral intervention. Special educators need to re-attend to providing services to students who have been identified as having disabilities (Pugach & Johnson, 1989; Ortiz, 1990b).

In 1981, Chalfant and Pysh recommended that TATs be formed of regular classroom teachers to facilitate prereferral problem solving. The TATs would involve special educators only for consultation. This intervention would be under the authority of the regular education system, not special education (Garcia & Ortiz, 1988). The team and the referring teacher would meet together to discuss problems, brainstorm solutions, and develop a plan of action, which would be implemented by the referring teacher with the support of team members. The team would conduct follow-up meetings to evaluate student progress and develop other instructional recommendations if necessary. The TAT would ultimately decide whether or not a formal referral to special education should be made (Garcia & Ortiz, 1988). The foremost benefit of the TAT would be the avoidance of long delays in obtaining assistance for teachers. Teachers would have the opportunity to meet with their colleagues daily to problem solve (Chalfant, Pysh, & Moultrie, 1979), as opposed to receiving delayed assistance from traditional special education intervention teams.

Gersten and Woodward (1990) have expressed their concerns about current prereferral intervention practices, pointing out that investigations by The Handicapped Minority Research Institutes of Texas and California found that when prereferral interventions did exist, they seldom included techniques that stimulated language acquisition. The schools serving students from language minority backgrounds demonstrated little awareness of issues in language development or comprehension strategy instruction (Gersten & Woodward, 1990). Garcia and Ortiz (1988) stated that errors in determining the educational needs of students with limited English proficiency occur most frequently when teachers and other school personnel lack an understanding of second language acquisition and educationally relevant cultural differences.

The at-risk or CLDE student could have learning and/or behavior problems that are due to external factors such as the learning environment, the teacher, or the curriculum. On the other hand, the learning or behavior problems could also be related to internal factors such as a language difference, a cultural difference, a disabling condition, or a combination of these factors. It is also likely that a combination of these factors need to be addressed within an ecological framework or intervention model.

A major goal of prereferral intervention is to identify and implement a series of instructional and behavioral interventions within the regular or bilingual/ESL classroom. Frequently the problem can be ameliorated at this level without the formal services of special education or bilingual special education. Differences in experiential background and previous school settings could be resolved by providing cognitive learning strategy interventions and curriculum modifications that are culturally and linguistically based. Difficulties stemming from acculturation stress could be resolved through cross-cultural counseling, peer support groups, or instruction in cultural survival techniques. Learning problems associated with limited English proficiency could be resolved by language development interventions such as ESL instruction, native language development, and bilingual assistance and instruction. At the very least, a high-risk student with cultural and linguistic differences should not be formally referred for special education services without first considering (a) time for adjustment, (b) familiarity with the school system and language, and (c) cultural differences. It is essential that more research be conducted to determine how classroom teachers actually decide to refer students to special education and what attempts they make at prereferral interventions prior to the formal referral.

Prereferral intervention has been identified as a major component of bilingual/cross-cultural special education. It should be noted, however, that the problems facing bilingual/multicultural special education are not unique to this new field but are related to major problems facing both regular and special education generally (Rueda, 1988). As Pugach and Johnson (1989) have pointed out, prereferral intervention merely represents one level of change needed if schools are to accommodate students with problems. Changes will also be required in school structure, teacher education, and school reform generally. According to Pugach and Johnson (1989), "Teachers need time to engage in the reflective process that skilled problem solving requires, time to step back from daily teaching pressures" (p. 225). Therefore, administrators need to provide flexible scheduling and allot time for teachers to collaborate (Ortiz & Garcia, 1988).

An issue of high priority for regular and bilingual administrators will increasingly be to create district-wide problem solving teams. A prereferral process should be in place in all schools for teachers to work together to solve student difficulties (Ortiz & Garcia, 1988). The benefits would be multiple. The process of prereferral intervention builds collaborative learning communities in schools and prereferral provides continuous staff development with regard to instructional strategies that can meet teachers' needs (Garcia & Ortiz, 1988). With this process in place, the needs of all students could be better accommodated in general education classrooms—a more cost-effective way of providing services than special education (Ortiz & Garcia, 1988).

Assessment

Assessment may be defined as the evaluation of all relevant aspects of a child's behavior and environment for the purposes of classifying the child for placement and acquiring information relevant to planning and subsequent evaluation (Oakland & Matuzek, 1977). It should be pointed out that assessment is broader than testing and as such encompasses informal and nonpsychometric approaches as well as standardized norm referenced modes of assessment. The issue of assessment has received the greatest degree of attention of all the topics in the field of bilingual special education (Ambert & Dew, 1982; Hamayan & Damico, 1991; Mowder, 1980; Plata, 1982). It can be divided into three separate areas: psychological assessment, language assessment, and educational assessment.

Psychological Assessment. Figueroa (1989) conducted an extensive review of the literature on psychological testing of students from minority backgrounds and stated that the existing practices in school psychology related to intelligence testing have not changed much over the past 70 years. The major findings he reported documented the following:

1. Nonverbal IQs were always higher than verbal IQs; nonverbal IQs were considered to be free of language and culture and hence to be measures of innate ability.

2. Nonverbal IQs were not found to be as effective in predicting academic achievement as verbal IQs.

3. The impact of bilingualism on test scores was consistently ignored.

4. The formal or informal translation of tests became the most desired solution (the complexities of translation were not understood).

5. Anomalous data on testing bilinguals has been systematically discarded. (Figueroa, 1989)

These findings are all predicated on and closely tied to a norm-referenced psychometric model. Attempts to correct or adapt this traditional model have failed. The best known and most significant of these efforts was undertaken by Mercer (1979), when she developed the System of Multicultural Pluralistic Assessment (SOMPA). Today, however, Mercer believes that the psychometric model is intrinsically flawed and cannot be successfully adapted for use with students from language minority backgrounds (Mercer, 1986).

Alternative assessment models have been presented over the last 2 decades in response to the inconsistencies found with students from minority backgrounds over the years (Mercer & Rueda, 1991). Mercer and Rueda have categorized the pervasive medical model of the 1960s as grounded in the functionalist/objectivist paradigm, in which "objectivity, standardization, norms, measurements, reliable classification are all primary values. Assessment focuses on commonalities. Individuals who do deviate markedly are defined as 'abnormal' and, at times, as 'disabled'" (p. 5). The functionalist/objectivist paradigm encompasses the medical model, the psychomedical model, and the cognitive model. This paradigm has had a profound impact on how disability is defined and understood and thus on how it is identified and measured through tests and assessment procedures. According to Mercer and Rueda, theoretical paradigms will continue to compete for acceptance in the 1990s. This implies that the assessment of language minority students will become more diverse rather than more unitary in the future.

Figueroa (1989) has challenged school psychologists to engage in a major paradigm shift or to continue to engage in what some consider to be malpractice. In effect, what is needed is movement toward new and dynamic models for measuring intelligence (Campione, Brown, & Ferrara, 1982; Duran, 1989). Figueroa (1989) has proposed a new model based on the information-processing research of Campione, Brown, and Ferrara (1982). These researchers believe that the building blocks of intelligence are speed of processing, knowledge base, strategies, metacognition, and executive control. According to Figueroa (1988), the use of these constructs requires a shift of focus from standardized psychometrics to modifications of learning environments such as the approach used by Feuerstein (1979) in the Learning Potential Assessment Device (LPAD). In this type of model, the growth from unassisted performance to mediated or assisted performance (Vygotsky's zone of proximal development) can be measured. For the student with limited English proficiency, this type of assessment is a much more accurate measure of the upper range of ability (Budoff, Gimon, & Corman, 1974; Ruiz, 1988).

Moll (1989) stated that Vygotsky developed the concept of the zone of proximal development partially to counteract the uses of traditional static assessment measures such as IQ tests to determine children's abilities. Moll interpreted the zone as "a way of building diversity into assessment practices" (p. 57). Use of the zone can serve as a precautionary measure against underestimating students' intellectual capabilities as assessed through traditional assessment techniques and observed in restrictive instructional conditions (Moll, 1989, p. 57).

Cummins (1984) reported that in one study of 400 students from minority backgrounds the majority of the psychological assessments conducted provided results that the psychologists themselves could not interpret confidently. Almost no sound diagnostic determinations about student potential could be drawn. Cummins further stated that psychologists in the study were reluctant to admit these results due to teacher expectations and pressure to maintain professional credibility. According to Cummins (1986), the data suggest that "the structure within which psychological assessment takes place orients the psychologist to locate the cause of the academic problem within the minority student" (p. 29).

Language Assessment. Language assessment of high-risk students is also of critical importance in bilingual/cross-cultural special education. Research in this area continues to document the difficulty that teachers and clinicians have in distinguishing between a language difference and a language disability (Cummins 1984; Langdon, 1989; Ortiz & Maldonado-Colon, 1986). The use of a standardized and discrete point language assessment approach has proved inadequate in assessing the dual language abilities of bilingual students (Bernstein, 1989; Langdon, 1989; Lee, 1989). Samora-Curry (1990) has suggested that if one hypothesizes or theorizes that language learning is facilitated by comprehensible input, in context-embedded situations with concrete referents available, then it is logical for the language assessment tools to be structured in the same way. As a result, a growing number of speech and language specialists advocate the use of nonstandardized and informal assessment alternatives for high-risk students from diverse language minority groups (Bernstein, 1989; Mattes & Omark, 1984; Oller, 1983). These approaches to language assessment utilize naturally generated language samples to assess language pragmatics or functional communicative competence. When a naturalistic approach is used for assessment, the language specialist can describe the quality of communication between the student and other speakers in a variety of contexts including the home and community. Cheng (1989) has developed a checklist that has been used successfully with Asian and other students from language minority backgrounds. Damico (1991) is also doing pioneering work along these lines.

Educational Assessment. Educational assessment could be viewed as the most important area of assessment of at-risk students because it is universal and pervasive and it is much more closely related or at least potentially related to instruction. Another reason for its importance is that it often occurs before language and psychological assessment. Because educational assessment generally occurs within the regular education context, prereferral intervention and student advocacy are potential benefits of this type of assessment. Regular education teachers can be helpful at the prereferral stage by collecting both formal and informal educational assessment data.

Item bias and norming bias have been discussed at length in the literature. Duran (1988) pointed out that existing testing practices are limited in validity and reliability for Hispanic students because of factors such as limited English proficiency, lack of familiarity with the content of the test items, lack of cultural sensitivity of the test administrators, and lack of test-taking strategies on the part of the students. Cummins (1984) has also shown that achievement tests do not provide specific feedback to teachers for instructional purposes.

Because of the limitations of norm-referenced tests, special educators have promoted the use of criterion-referenced and curriculum-based assessment instruments and procedures, which provide more instructional direction to both teachers and students. It is perhaps for this reason, as well as because of its availability in Spanish, that the Brigance (1983) has become so popular for bilingual special educators. However, Duran (1989) indicated that even these types of instruments and approaches are limited because they are not based on explicit cognitive processing models of learning that offer "on-line" advice to students during the very act of learning. In an attempt to provide a more effective educational testing approach, Duran (1989) called for the use of a dynamic assessment approach he referred to as "reciprocal teaching" (p. 156). Dynamic assessment establishes a strong link between testing and teaching. It utilizes a test-teach-test procedure that encourages the teacher to be a diagnostician who uses clinical judgment in the evaluation of student performance.

Appropriate Instruction

Instructional approaches and strategies for culturally and linguistically different students with exceptionalities can be drawn from three theoretical perspectives for bilingual/multicultural special education: prevention, integration of theory into practice, and instructional strategies.

For the past several years, Cummins (1984, 1986, 1989) has argued that minority student underachievement is primarily a sociohistorical outcome of discriminatory treatment in society as well as in the public schools. He sees special education for minority students with mild disabilities more as an outcome of this unequal treatment than as a valid educational construct or program, thereby making a strong case for the educational empowerment of students from language minority groups and their parents. His bilingual special education framework calls for schools and educators to stop disabling students from minority backgrounds and to start empowering them by promoting their linguistic talents, personal identities, and ability to succeed academically. His empowerment model includes the following four dimensions (Cummins, 1986, p. 24):

1. An additive rather than a subtractive incorporation of the students' language and culture.

2. A collaborative rather than an exclusionary approach to parent and community involvement.

3. An interactive and experiential as opposed to a transmission-oriented pedagogy.

4. An advocacy-oriented rather than a legitimization-oriented assessment process.

Cummins (1986) has stated that considerable research data suggest that the inclusion of minority students' language and culture into the school program is a significant predictor of academic success. According to Cummins, educators who take an additive instructional approach give merit to students' native linguistic and cultural repertoires and view instruction as adding a second language to existing competency. This additive approach is likely to empower students more than a subtractive approach in which instruction is viewed as replacing or subtracting a student's primary language and culture.

Fradd (1987) has expanded on the differentiation between additive and subtractive bilingual learning environments by further distinguishing them as remedial and developmental programs. According to Fradd, remedial programs are designed to remedy problems, whereas developmental language programs are intended to enhance students' linguistic skills. When students are viewed as lacking in basic ability because they lack English proficiency, remediation is recommended. The difference in the approaches is often determined by the attitude of the teacher as much as the instructional plan. If students' native language competency and culture are valued, they will be used to add English. In this manner, the experience of the student with linguistic and cultural differences will be developmental and additive (Fradd, 1987).

The major goal of Fradd's theoretical framework and empowerment model is to prevent the need for special education for students from minority backgrounds as much as possible. The implementation of this model will require major changes in the way special education is currently conceived and delivered.

Research by Samora-Curry (1990) found that an increased amount of English spoken in the home did not help the language of bilingual students with exceptionalities; it actually hampered it. She suggested that parents need to develop stronger first language skills prior to introducing the second language, English. Her study indicated this as critical for students who have mental retardation. Yet, parent interaction with their children in the home through the first language is frequently regarded by educators as contributing to academic difficulties (Cummins, 1984).

Ruiz (1989), in her discussion of the development of the Optimal Learning Environment Curriculum (OLE), described an extensive literature review that generated important instructional principles for CLDE students. They are as follows:

1. Take into account students' sociocultural backgrounds and their effects on oral language, reading and writing, and second language learning.

2. Take into account students' possible learning disabilities and their effects on oral language, reading and writing, and second language learning.

3. Follow developmental process in literacy acquisition.

4. Locate curriculum in a meaningful context in which the communicative purpose is clear and authentic.

5. Connect curriculum with the students' personal experiences.

6. Incorporate children's literature into reading, writing, and ESL lessons.

7. Involve parents as active partners in the instruction of their children.

8. Give students experience with whole texts in reading, writing, and ESL lessons.

9. Incorporate collaborative learning whenever possible. (p. 134)

Teachers need to provide instruction that integrates collaborative, interactive, and meaningful instructional approaches for students who are linguistically and culturally different. Research by The Texas and California Handicapped Minority Research Institute found that special education classes that are most successful with minority students who have mild disabilities are those that resemble good bilingual education classes. These classes were described as whole language oriented, incorporating comprehensible input, cooperative learning, and student empowerment (Figueroa, Fradd, & Correa, 1989). The AIM for the BESt project findings indicate that the use of interactive instructional approaches results in genuine student involvement; improvement in students' reading vocabulary and comprehension and oral and written skills; and increased self-confidence and self-esteem (Rivera, 1990).

Moll (1989) has suggested that whole activity and mediation, two aspects of Vygotsky's zone of proximal development, are important considerations for writing instruction for second language learners. According to Moll, Vygotsky insisted that instruction be presented in "whole activities." Learning should not be broken down into separate parts; instead, it should be divided into units that contain all the basic characteristics of the whole subject. Instruction that assumes that students who are limited in English need to master lower level skills before being involved in higher level thinking activities is misguided. Cummins (1984) affirmed this with reading. He stated that the exclusion of cognitive strategies and higher order thinking skills in reading instruction harms the ability of students from language minority backgrounds to achieve academic and language competence. For writing instruction, this implies that the goal should be to collaboratively communicate information from whole activities, not isolated skills for practice. According to Moll, instruction must also strategically organize mediation. Within the interactions of the teacher, students, and peers, knowledge is transferred. Situations for learning occur when people interact. The zone of proximal development is created socially in the interaction of collaborative activity (Moll, 1989).

Presently, there is a lack of substantial research in mathematics education for CLDE students in special education. Leon (1991) stated that language and culture should have a central role in the design of mathematics programs for bilingual special education students. She suggested that language, vocabulary, and decision making need to be emphasized in mathematical word problems.

Cooperative learning is often proposed for use with students from language minority backgrounds, as well as with other at-risk students (Calderon, 1989). Cooperative learning encompasses a wide range of teaching strategies and may be used for whole language approaches, ESL and transition into English, sheltered instruction and critical thinking, developing cognitive and metacognitive strategies, and classrooms with few LEP students (Calderon, 1989).

Baca and Cervantes (1989) proposed a theoretical framework for bilingual special education that integrates relevant research and validated practices from the parent disciplines of regular, bilingual, and special education. This synthesis is translated into the following instructional guidelines for bilingual special education:

1. A clear sense of mission regarding bilingual/multicultural special education is shared by all staff members.

2. Strong and effective leadership is provided for the bilingual/multicultural special education program.

3. High expectations are established for all teachers and students in the program.

4. Effective home-school support systems are established.

5. Native language instruction as well as ESL instruction are included in all IEPs as appropriate.

6. Teachers mediate instruction, monitor student progress, and provide frequent feedback using both the first and the second languages as appropriate.

7. Instruction focuses on the students' abilities and needed learning strategies.

8. Special instruction considers the students' cultural backgrounds by using experiences drawn from the community.

9. The students' primary language skills are developed up to the cognitive and academic level needed to attain similar advanced English language skills.

10. Special instruction is provided by appropriately trained bilingual/multicultural special education staff.

11. Time on task and task completion are encouraged in the least restrictive environment.

12. All students, all languages, and all cultures are treated with equal respect.

13. All staff must believe that bilingual/multicultural education is effective in raising the achievement levels of LEP students with disabilities. (pp. 94–95)

Native language and culture, along with ESL programs and multicultural education strategies, should be provided in special education programs. Educators should develop adequate bilingual and ESL programs to serve bilingual children with exceptionalities (Whitaker & Prieto, 1989). Richard-Amato (1988) described an optimal program for ESL students as one that combines ESL instruction with mainstreaming, sheltered classes, and maintenance bilingual education. Highly specialized programs for LEP students with exceptionalities can be formed by integrating the expertise of special education and bilingual/ESL education (Cloud, 1988).

Baca (1990) has pointed out that teaching English and the native language is important, but it should not become the primary objective. Instruction should assist the student to reach his or her maximum potential for learning. Both intensive native language instruction and the reinforcement of cultural identity appear to enhance the cognitive and academic development of students who are linguistically and culturally different (Cummins, 1986).

IEPs should specify the language of instruction (Ambert & Dew, 1982; Whitaker & Prieto, 1989). The language of instruction for bilingual children with exceptionalities should be consistent with what is known about relationships between the native and second language (Whitaker & Prieto, 1989). Effective IEPs for LEP students with exceptionalities should account for all of the students' basic educational needs, including the need for ESL instruction (Cloud, 1988).

It should also be noted that the guidelines for operationalizing a bilingual/multicultural special education curriculum and program are further defined when molded to specific areas of disability. The ingredients for a bilingual/multicultural special education program need to be combined with instructional techniques tailored to each area of disability. General guidelines for instructing students who have visual impairments, hearing impairments, learning impairments, speech impairments, or emotional disturbances should be taken into consideration.

Just how the bilingual special education instruction would be implemented could vary considerably. By law and sound pedagogical practice, it should occur in the least restrictive environment and in the spirit of inclusion. This generally means within the mainstream educational environment to the extent possible. The CLDE student could be served in a regular monolingual or bilingual classroom, in a resource room, or, occasionally and if needed, in a self-contained classroom or special facility. The major determinants of the program design and delivery mode would be first the needs of the student and second the availability of specially trained bilingual, ESL, and bilingual/multicultural special education personnel. Finally, curriculum materials would have to be acquired and or adapted from a native language and ESL perspective.

3. Implications for Administrators

Both regular and special education administrators must collaborate with one another and with teachers to design and implement programs that are based on research reviews and empirical studies. Particular emphasis should be given to improving prereferral services and inservice training.

Based on the rationale, assumptions, and research synthesis previously discussed, this section focuses on the implications for program planning, design, and implementation. Of particular interest are the specific roles and responsibilities that administrators should be prepared to assume in order to design and implement high-quality programs and services for CLDE students. Before moving into the specific guidelines and suggestions for administrators, it may be useful to discuss briefly the three basic principles upon which these guidelines are based. They are intended to provide guidance and direction for both program planners and the teachers who will actually instruct these students.

The first principle is that prevention is the highest priority. Since prevention is broadly conceived here, it has several meanings. First is the idea of preventing physical and psychological disabilities by improving the quality of life and education for language minority communities. Early intervention provides a means of preventing or reducing the degree of impact of a disability. Finally, prevention is viewed as a way of empowering students from language minority backgrounds early in their lives so that they do not develop disabilities as a result of poor or inappropriate instruction or the lack of a culturally and linguistically responsive learning environment.

The second principle is that once appropriate prereferral instructional alternatives for students with limited English proficiency have been attempted without success, then and only then should formal assessment and testing be initiated. These assessment procedures should be valid, reliable, and culturally and linguistically responsive. They should emphasize the informal and dynamic aspects of assessment.

The third principle that should guide program design and implementation is that special education services for CLDE students should be framed in the cultural and linguistic context that is optimal for each student's maximum cognitive and affective development. This, in effect, implies that special education is only really special and appropriate for culturally and linguistically diverse students when it utilizes the native language and culture along with ESL and multicultural education strategies. The IEPs of these students should reflect this important principle and should include IEP goals and objectives related to the language and cultural context of their learning needs and learning styles.

Based on the research review and synthesis as well as on state-of-the-art best practices, school administrators have the opportunity to provide the vision and strong leadership that is needed for implementing high-quality services for CLDE students and their families. These issues were almost unheard of in the education community 20 years ago. Today they are receiving increased attention from scholars as well as practitioners.

If today's schools are going to be successful in meeting the needs of LEP students with disabilities, school administrators will have to emphasize prevention. They will have to concentrate on promoting the policies and instructional environments that help prevent disabilities from having their maximum negative impact on students.

School principals should provide the leadership that will help reduce inappropriate referrals of students from language minority backgrounds to special education. This is perhaps best accomplished by regular education child study and intervention teams through prereferral interventions. This can maximize the achievement levels of culturally and linguistically different students and reduce their overrepresentation in special education.

Prereferral

Administrators should attend to the time general educators need to explore and demonstrate their ability to meet diverse needs in their classrooms. Prereferral intervention efforts are at risk if the management of schools does not incorporate specific structures that routinely allow teachers to collaborate.

Collaboration between regular and special education administrators will strengthen regular education programs for students with limited English proficiency in both native language instruction and ESL services. This collaboration should focus on establishing policy, revising curriculum, and providing inservice training as well as the planning time needed to better prepare and involve regular classroom teachers in the prereferral process as it relates to these students. This could involve establishing partnerships and sharing human and financial resources with regular education and other categorical programs.

Fradd (1987) noted that *The Harvard Education Letter* of 1986 affirmed that administrators can do a great deal to foster a climate of mutual sharing and collaboration. Administrators can provide guidance and leadership to parents and other community members so additional assistance can be provided in creating programs that benefit students with disabilities.

Administrators must also be sensitive to the fact that prereferral intervention committees may recommend instructional strategies that are unfamiliar to some referring teachers. In these cases, referring teachers will need inservice training or demonstration by a colleague (Ortiz, 1990b). Findings from the AIM for the BESt project support this implication. According to Ortiz (1990b), S/TAT teams helped identify problems and areas of training for schools. Ortiz suggested that "principals should analyze the nature of problems referred to the team to determine areas in which teachers seem to need the most help" (p. 4). The documented needs could be used to plan staff-development activities on campuses or across school districts. School policy may also be affected as patterns in findings appear (Ortiz, 1990b).

Assessment

Administrators will need to be aware of the multiple assessment paradigms that exist and acknowledge teachers' differing views on assessment practices. In a particular school, special educators working side by side may have differing approaches to assessment. The administrator should respect each practitioner's approach. Teachers who begin to incorporate informal assessments will need support in terms of time constraints. When time is committed to informal assessment, it may no longer be possible to abide by the previous time schedule used with standardized tests. Pressure to continue to administer complete standardized batteries may jeopardize a teacher's efforts to administer and develop informal assessments.

Training in informal assessment will increasingly become an issue of high priority for administrators. Informal assessment, supported by research, is contextual and is student-advocacy oriented. Cummins (1986) has suggested an alternative role for psychologists and special educators—that of advocate. Instead of legitimizing disabilities in assessment, psychologists and special educators should critically examine the educational experiences that have been offered to students (Cummins, 1986).

Administrators should encourage the increased use of informal and dynamic assessment procedures as opposed to relying heavily on standardized psychometric procedures. This will result in a more holistic, instructionally relevant, and equitable assessment. This type of assessment has been an elusive goal throughout the history of special education. The assessment of culturally and linguistically diverse students has been a major concern of parents, professionals, and legislators, as evidenced by the inclusion of a nonbiased assessment provision in the Education for All Handicapped Children Act of 1975 and its 1991 reauthorization known as the Individuals with Disabilities Education Act (IDEA).

The assessment of children with special needs has been such a driving concern for special educators that it has consumed an inordinate amount of our professional energy and nearly half of our available financial resources. Despite this level of commitment, the end result has been, to a great extent, assessment for legal, regulatory, and administrative reasons, as opposed to assessment for instructional purposes. Current efforts to reform assessment should strive to make it student centered and advocacy oriented, as well as integrally related to instruction.

Special education and/or bilingual special education directors should establish assessment policies and procedures that ensure that LEP students' native languages and cultures are included in a dynamic assessment process such as the Optimal Learning Environment (OLE) project (Figueroa, 1989) or the AIM for the BESt project (Ortiz, Yates, & Garcia, 1990). This also implies that directors should actively recruit more bilingual assessment personnel as well as provide continued inservice training to present staff who are engaged in the various facets of bilingual student assessment. Movement toward more informal and dynamic assessment procedures should be given more emphasis by directors than the use of static, standardized psychometric procedures.

Appropriate Instruction

Special education administrators should advocate for special education services for CLDE students that prioritize the need for native language instruction, development, and reinforcement along with ESL services that provide comprehensible English input in the instructional content areas. Administrators should also require that the IEPs of these students reflect the student language and cultural strengths as well as their needs and learning styles.

Directors of special education and/or bilingual education, along with program supervisors, should plan and implement a flexible instructional delivery system that incorporates a continuum of bilingual/-multicultural and/or ESL services. In order to do this, immediate attention must be given to additional recruitment of bilingual special education specialists and bilingual paraprofessionals. Staff development will also be necessary as special education personnel continue to move into collaborative and inclusion-oriented delivery models.

Administrators need to work to include the culture and community of students with exceptionalities into school programs. Involvement of parents from minority groups should be a priority in order to provide support for students and their teachers. These parents often do not have sufficient information on how to help their children academically, and they are not included in school activities (Cummins, 1984). "When educators involve minority parents as partners in their children's education, parents appear to develop a sense of efficacy that communicates itself to children, with positive academic consequences" (Cummins, 1986, p. 26). Efforts to provide parents with channels in which they are genuinely valued, encouraged, and guided in having a positive impact on their children's school success create such an atmosphere.

Administrators should emphasize the need for advanced specialized training of all staff who work with LEP children with disabilities. Few special educators are trained to work with this group of students, and no coherent curriculum has been developed (Baca & Cervantes, 1989; Fradd, 1987). Nonetheless, the needs of these students should be addressed in all aspects of program development, including staff development. The public schools' difficulty in meeting the needs of bilingual students with exceptionalities is due primarily to a lack of qualified personnel. Administrators should identify these shortcomings and make them priorities for future planning. Needs have to be acknowledged and identified before services can be provided.

Administrators will have to collaborate to make it possible for all teachers to provide appropriate instruction for children from minority groups in special education. All personnel involved, including special education teachers, speech and language therapists, classroom teachers, school psychologists, and social workers, need to be adequately trained in order to provide CLDE students with instruction that reflects the current thinking on effective teaching of this group. Students with linguistic and cultural differences need optimal opportunities for language and cognitive growth.

Proficiency in the native language of another culture does not automatically qualify a person to be a teacher of students in that language (Krashen, 1982). If special educators are going to provide relevant support to students from language minority groups and their teachers they must be adequately trained. They must be knowledgeable in the use of effective strategies for enhancing language acquisition and comprehension for second language learners, and they must have an understanding of cultural differences and their implications for effective instructional practice (Gersten & Woodward, 1990). Appropriate materials, as well as trained personnel, are essential to maximizing the success of children with exceptionalities for whom English is a second language (Cloud, 1988).

4. Implications for Teachers

Teachers are the most valuable resource in bilingual/ multicultural special education. When they are empowered with current instructional research information and the latest intervention strategies, they can facilitate the optimal cognitive and affective development of culturally and linguistically different exceptional students.

This section focuses on what prereferral intervention, assessment, and instruction mean in terms of teacher practices for students who have linguistic and cultural differences. These three areas, which are pertinent to both general and special educators, are becoming the responsibility of each and every educator. Prereferral intervention, which is becoming the jurisdiction of general educators, involves appropriate assessment of student language proficiency and dominance, instructional achievement, and cultural influences. These components are necessary for providing appropriate curriculum interventions. Prereferral intervention must ensure the implementation of procedures that are linguistically and culturally responsive. Language and cultural differences must be distinguished from learning disabilities prior to a referral for special education intervention. Assessments conducted by special educators must be conducted with full consideration of the second language and cultural issues addressed in prereferral. Instruction offered to a culturally and linguistically different student with a confirmed disability should utilize strategies that address both the disability and the cultural and linguistic learning differences, involving both general educators and special educators in providing appropriate instruction.

Prereferral Intervention

The pervasive overrepresentation of students from language minority backgrounds in special education programs warrants the need for a comprehensive inclusion of a prereferral process in public schools. Without alternative programs to special education intervention, the misidentification and misplacement of these students into special education programs will continue. Students with cultural and linguistic differences bring distinct needs to the classroom. For those who do not have disabilities, it is critical to have their educational needs met within general education classrooms. Unless educators are able to identify and accommodate students' second language and multicultural needs, the excessive use of special education will persist.

Prereferral intervention has the potential to provide teachers with a resource that assists in meeting diverse student needs outside of special education. At present, programs that offer continual assistance to classroom teachers to accommodate learning differences are scarce, often involving long waiting lists and insufficient consultative time for teachers and students needing immediate assistance. Furthermore, while special educators are trained in accommodating differences related to learning disabilities, they are not trained to deal with language and cultural diversity. Special educators' consultative time with teachers who have students with disabilities is already limited. Moreover, alternatives to special education placement are extremely limited.

Prereferral intervention can reduce inappropriate referrals to special education by (a) training teachers to distinguish learning differences from learning disabilities and (b) introducing instructional strategies that are successful with students who have cultural and linguistic differences. Prereferral intervention also provides an alternative program to special education that (a) provides ongoing assistance to classroom teachers to meet the learning needs of these students and (b) serves as an ongoing assistance program for all students who do not have disabilities but could benefit from educational strategies that are successful with students with cultural and linguistic differences.

The prereferral process requires that all teachers become skilled in distinguishing between language and cultural differences and learning problems. The education of students with cultural and linguistic difference rests in the hands of regular educators, bilingual educators, and ESL instructors. It is critical for bilingual and ESL teachers—those who are versed in second language and multicultural issues—to take the lead in the prereferral intervention process. Their leadership and commitment are required in order to establish prereferral intervention as a structured and ongoing alternative program in public schools.

Regular, bilingual, ESL, and special educators all have expertise to offer, given the structured time in which to share it. It is important to point out that the prereferral process acknowledges and respects the capability of classroom teachers given adequate exposure to and training in second language learning and multicultural issues. The sharing of special educators' experience with students with diverse learning abilities is invaluable and should be offered at the request of the prereferral team. The involvement of regular educators is of utmost importance because their role as ESL instructors is increasing due to the growing diversity of the regular classroom. The leadership should be maintained by general classroom teachers so that, to the extent possible, interventions occur in general education classrooms.

Prereferral interventions must be linguistically and culturally responsive. They should be based on current research on the learning of students from language minority backgrounds. Therefore, training in second language learning and multicultural instructional strategies must occur within the prereferral intervention process. The AIM for the BESt project (Ortiz, 1990a) conducted a 1-day training session for team members in which the purpose and procedures to be followed by the team were discussed (e.g., procedures for conducting meetings, record keeping and problem-solving strategies). Special education, bilingual education, and ESL teachers received 1-day training on shared literature and process-oriented writing (Ortiz, 1990a).

Prereferral intervention is a structure by which educators can problem solve collaboratively as skilled professionals to meet the diverse needs of their students. Time for communication is a critical element, and it must be structured into the school day. The problem-solving teams in the AIM for the BESt project (Ortiz, 1990a) set a regular meeting time and met only when a teacher requested assistance. All meetings were held after school (Ortiz, 1990a). The structure of the AIM for the BESt project involved a Request for Assistance packet developed by the problem solving teams. Their general operating procedures were as follows:

1. The teacher requesting assistance submitted a completed packet to the team coordinator.

2. The coordinator requested all other school personnel in regular contact with the student to complete a behavior checklist and return it to him/her within a week.

3. The coordinator then developed a composite checklist and distributed it to the team members.

4. A [30-minute problem-solving] team meeting was held to discuss student needs and to determine the best plan of action for the student. [One or two objectives were negotiated.]

5. An intervention plan was developed which was then implemented by the teacher or other service provider.

6. A follow-up meeting was held to review progress and to develop additional interventions if necessary. (p. 4)

The *EAC-WEST News* (Wilde, 1991), produced by the Bilingual Education Evaluation Assistance Center, Western Region, has suggested the following procedures in prereferral models:

Gather information on language proficiency/dominance, including the effectiveness of the curriculum for language minority students; other records of the student's work including observations, work samples, interviews with parents [and] other teachers; and other testing if necessary.

Collaborate with professional peers to review the child's cultural, linguistic and experiential background; level of acculturation; sociolinguistic development; and cognitive learning styles. Also assess the teacher's instructional style, sequencing of instruction, language of instruction, and coordination with other programs. Determine whether interventions in the regular education classroom can ameliorate the problem for the student.

Determine whether additional services may be available to help the student; e.g., Chapter I, Title VII, ESL and special tutoring. These services, provided within the regular classroom context, may be sufficient to enhance the student's success.

Provide psychosocial assistance such as cross-cultural counseling, acculturation support groups, "survival skills" training, and peer tutors. These support services might be provided on a pull-out basis, after school, or through the school counselor.

Ensure that the student is receiving appropriate [native language] and [second language] assistance. Perhaps moving the child to a different classroom in which the teacher is more familiar with [the native language], or s/he teaches with a more ESL-type approach, would help the child. (p. 4)

Garcia & Ortiz (1988) have developed a prereferral process model for intervention as shown in Figure 2.

Assessment

When, through the prereferral process, learning difficulties cannot be attributed to cultural and linguistic differences and learning problems are still suspected, a referral for special education intervention is appropriate. Assessments should be conducted with full consideration of second language and cultural issues. Although the prereferral process may find that a student's learning difficulty is not attributable to cultural and linguistic differences, a learning disability should not be assumed. Special educators should keep in mind the criticisms standardized assessments have received in regard to testing of students from minority groups. Their assessment process must be culturally and linguistically responsive so that it does not result in inappropriate placements.

FIGURE 2
Preventing Inappropriate Placements of Language Minority Students in Special Education: A Prereferral Process

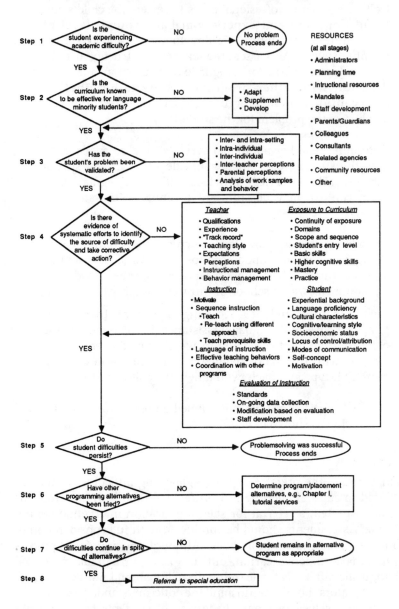

Note. From "Preventing Inappropriate Referrals of Language Minority Students to Special Education" by S. Garcia & A. Ortiz, 1988, *New Focus, 5,* p. 3. The National Clearinghouse for Bilingual Education Occasional Papers in Bilingual Education.

The paradigms under which special educators assess children from minority groups for special education placement must be considered. The medical model within the functionalist/objectivist paradigm is strongly based in standardization, norms, and measurements (Mercer & Rueda, 1991). Special educators should examine the validity of the assessments used with students who have cultural and linguistic differences. A standardized testing orientation for these students is not appropriate. As addressed in the Research Synthesis section, standardized tests have historically proved inadequate in assessing the abilities of students from minority groups, and special educators must incorporate alternative assessments for them. Any standardized testing should be interpreted cautiously and should not be the sole basis for special education placement decisions.

Informal assessment, which includes all measures that are not standardized or norm referenced (Ambert & Dew, 1982), should be incorporated into assessment agendas for minority students. Time will have to be appropriated for this. It is unrealistic to expect that a special educator will have sufficient time to administer the traditional battery of standardized tests plus informal assessments, especially in both the native language and English. Excessive and unrealistic testing agendas are carried out at the expense of teaching time. This must be avoided whenever possible.

Assessment conducted within special education for a student with cultural and linguistic differences must take into consideration the same student variables addressed in the prereferral process (see Figure 3). These variables are considerations at Step 4 in the prereferral process described in Figure 2 (Garcia & Ortiz, 1988). A student's (a) experiential background, (b) culture, (c) language proficiency, (d) learning style, and (e) motivational influences are all important considerations for a special education evaluation. The selection of assessment instruments and their interpretation must be responsive to the whole student.

The following examples of informal measures are drawn from Oller's (1979) discussion of discrete point versus integrative testing (cited in Richard-Amato, 1988). These measures are intended to provide attention to meaningful context with normal uses of language, in contrast to discrete point tests, which, according to Oller (1979) involve "rote recital or manipulation of sequences of material without attention to meaning" (cited in Richard-Amato, 1988, p. 374). The appropriate use and selection of alternative assessment measures require training and exposure to a wide spectrum of measures that are considered informal. Implementation of informal assessment techniques should be done with a specific purpose and strategy.

FIGURE 3
Student Variables

Experiential Background
- Are there any factors in the student's school history which may be related to the current difficulty?
attendance/mobility
opportunities to learn
program placement(s)
quality of prior instruction
- Are there any variables related to family history which may have affected school performance?
lifestyle
length of residence in the U.S.
stress (e.g., poverty, lack of emotional support)
- Are there any variables related to the student's medical history which may have affected school performance?

vision	nutrition	illness
hearing	trauma or injury	

Culture
- How is the student's cultural background different from the culture of the school and larger society? (Mattes & Omark, 1984; Saville-Troike, 1978)
family (family size and structure, roles, responsibilities, expectations)
aspirations (success, goals)
language and communication (rules for adult, adult-child, child-child communication, language use at home, non-verbal communication)
religion (dietary restrictions, role expectations)
traditions and history (contact with homeland, reason for immigration)
decorum and discipline (standards for acceptable behavior)
- To what extent are the student's characteristics representative of the larger group?
continuum of culture (traditional, dualistic, atraditional [Ramírez & Castañeda, 1974])
degree of acculturation or assimilation
- Is the student able to function successfully in more than one cultural setting?
- Is the student's behavior culturally appropriate?

Language Proficiency
- Which is the student's dominant language? Which is the preferred?
settings (school, playground, home, church, etc.)
topics (academic subjects, day-to-day interactions)
speakers (parents, teachers, siblings, peers, etc.)
aspects of each language (syntax, vocabulary, phonology, use)
expressive vs. receptive
- What is the student's level of proficiency in the primary language and in English? (Cummins, 1984)
interpersonal communication skills
cognitive/academic literacy-related skills

FIGURE 3 - Continued

- Are the styles of verbal interaction used in the primary language different from those most valued at school, in English? (Heath, 1986)
  label quests (e.g., what's this? who?)
  meaning quests (adult infers for child, interprets or asks for explanation)
  accounts (generated by teller, information new to listener; e.g., show & tell, creative writing)
  eventcasts (running narrative on events as they unfold, or forecast of events in preparation)
  stories
- If so, has the student been exposed to those that are unfamiliar to him/her?
- What is the extent and nature of exposure to each language?
  What language(s) do the parents speak to each other?
  What language(s) do the parents speak to the child?
  What language(s) do the children use with each other?
  What television programs are seen in each language?
  Are stories read to the child? In what language(s)?
- Are student behaviors characteristic of second language acquisition?
- What types of language intervention has the student received?
  bilingual vs. monolingual instruction
  language development, enrichment, remediation
  additive vs. subtractive bilingualism (transition versus maintenance)

Learning Style

- Does the student's learning style require curricular/instructional accommodation?
  perceptual style differences (e.g., visual vs. auditory learner)
  cognitive style differences (e.g., inductive vs. deductive thinking)
  preferred style of participation (e.g., teacher vs. student directed, small vs. large group)
- If so, were these characteristics accommodated, or were alternative styles taught?

Motivational Influences

- Is the student's self-concept enhanced by school experiences?
  school environment communicates respect for culture and language
  student experiences academic and social success
- Is schooling perceived as relevant and necessary for success in the student's family and community?
  aspirations
  realistic expectations based on community experience
  culturally different criteria for success
  education perceived by the community as a tool for assimilation

Note. From "Preventing Inappropriate Referrals of Language Minority Students to Special Education" by S. Garcia & A. Ortiz, 1988, *New Focus, 5*, p. 7. The National Clearinghouse for Bilingual Education Occasional Papers in Bilingual Education.

Dictation

A sequence of words or phrases [is] selected from normal prose, or dialogue, or some other natural form of discourse to be dictated. This material is presented orally in sequences that are long enough to challenge short-term memory. *Skills assessed:* "processing of temporally constrained sequences of material in the [given] language and . . . dividing up the stream of speech and writing down what is heard requires understanding the meaning of the material." (p. 375)

Cloze Procedure

One variety of this technique involves deleting every fifth, sixth, or seventh word from a passage of prose. Each deleted word is replaced by a blank, and the examinee is asked to fill in the blanks to restore the missing words. Other varieties of this test may involve the deleting of specific vocabulary items, parts of speech, affixes, or particular types of grammatical markers within a passage or prose. *Skills Assessed:* "The examinee must utilize information that is inferred about the facts, events, ideas, relationships, states of affairs, social settings . . . contained in the passage." (p. 375)

Combined Cloze and Dictation

The examinee reads material from which certain portions have been deleted and simultaneously (or subsequently) hears the same material without deletions either live or on tape. The examinee's task is to fill in the missing portions the same as in the usual cloze procedure, but he has the added support of the auditory signal to help fill in the missing portions. Variations of this procedure . . . single words, or even parts of words, or sequences of words, or even whole sentences or longer segments may be deleted. The less material one deletes, the more the task resembles the standard cloze procedure, and the more one deletes, the more the task looks like a standard dictation. (p. 377)

Oral Cloze Procedure

The cloze passage is carefully prepared on a tape recording of the material with numbers read in for the blanks, or with pauses where blanks occur. It is also possible to read the material up to the blank, give the examinee the opportunity to guess the missing word, record the response, and at that point tell the examinee the right answer . . . or continue without any immediate feedback . . . Another procedure is to arrange the deletions so they always come at the end of a clause or sentence. Any of these cloze techniques [has] the advantage of being usable with nonliterate populations. (p. 377)

Oral Interview
The examinee is given the opportunity to talk. The evaluation may be only the subjective impression of the teacher or rating scales can be set to score certain student linguistic capabilities.

Composition or Essay Writing
This may involve a writing task where the examinee selects a topic and develops it, or where the teacher selects a passage and asks the examinee to fill in the blanks (requiring open ended responses, sentences or phrases).

Damico and Hamayan (1991) have suggested that the implementation of alternative assessment will occur in two stages. Stage one will involve gaining acceptance. Initially, teachers need to gain support from school administrators, other personnel involved in assessment, and teachers. The school principal is an important person from whom to gain support, as are special education and assessment supervisors and bilingual, ESL, and Title VII coordinators or supervisors. Teachers may also work to gain acceptance by presenting the need for alternative approaches to all people involved. Teachers can share facts about the limitations and bias in standardized testing for students with linguistic and cultural differences. Teachers can also demonstrate alternative approaches by linking an alternative assessment procedure with a traditional measure that can be presented in assessment reports to the special education committee. Hamayan and Damico have stressed that suggestions of alternative approaches need to be "well-prepared, clear, and nonthreatening" (p. 311). Furthermore, they have advised the teacher to be flexible and patient. Even after staff agree on the need for change, a transitional period is most likely to occur before changes are accepted and implemented.

Stage two involves effective implementation. Once alternative assessment is accepted, dissemination of information and training will be necessary. Specific and clear information on alternative assessment should be disseminated through inservice training sessions. Alternative approaches should be established and used effectively.

Instruction
Instruction for CLDE students is based mostly on research that describes optimal learning environments and instruction for second language learners. A specific body of knowledge of instructional intervention for bilingual students in special education is emerging. Research literature

continues to promote adherence to providing services in the least restrictive environment.

Students' need for native language and ESL instruction should be documented on their IEPs. The IEPs should reflect instructional strategies for second language learners and adaptations for the disabling conditions involved for all educational services to be provided. It is critical that the bilingual special education curriculum materials be linked to the core curriculum used in the classrooms. Bilingual special education students need a curriculum that is coordinated between special and classroom instructors and paraprofessionals if they are to receive maximum benefit.

There are three instructional models within which culturally and linguistically different students with disabilities can be served (Ambert & Dew, 1982).

The Bilingual Support Model. Within this model, monolingual English special education teachers are teamed with native language tutors/paraprofessionals to provide special education services. The native language paraprofessional works under the direction of the special educator. Training for native language tutors is imperative; they play important instructional roles in the provision of special education services. The special education teacher should provide ESL instruction.

The Coordinated Service Model. In this situation, CLDE students are served by a monolingual English-speaking special education teacher and a bilingual educator. The special education teacher is responsible for providing ESL instruction and implementing the IEP objectives in English. The bilingual teacher provides academic instruction in the native language. Here, the bilingual teacher takes leadership in special interventions. The special educator provides support to ensure that native language instruction is adapted to accommodate the learning disability. The special education teacher provides ESL instruction and takes greater responsibility for carrying out the IEP when the student is transitioned into all-English instruction.

The Integrated Bilingual Special Education Model. This model is used when teachers are available who are trained to serve students with disabilities and can also provide both native language and ESL for students with disabilities who also have cultural and linguistic differences. The bilingual special educator is responsible for the implementation of the IEP. Appropriate training of teachers hired for this position would involve study in providing services for students who have both disabilities and limited English proficiency.

Coordination among the service providers within these models is extremely important. All instructors involved in providing instructional services to a CLDE student need to collaborate on instructional and behavioral strategies. This would include special educators, native language tutors/paraprofessionals, classroom teachers, ESL teachers, and specialty teachers (e.g., art, music, PE). Parents should also be included as service providers. Parent participation in extending school efforts into the home should be requested. It is important that a consistent program, one that is responsive to special learning, behavioral, linguistic, and cultural needs, be provided to the CLDE student.

Instruction provided for CLDE students incorporates techniques and approaches that have been found by research to be optimal for students from language minority groups. Willig and Ortiz (1991) have addressed effective instruction for individual educational programming. Effective instruction for students from language minority groups stresses "that language learners are active learners who when exposed to sufficient language input from others, devise hypotheses about rules, test them out, modify them, and gradually construct their own language" (p. 291). Material that is meaningful and contextual should be offered. It is also important that "the materials used and the instructional strategies themselves be well-structured, student-initiated, highly motivating, progress in a sequential fashion, and make use of the learner's expectancies regarding the consequences of interaction" (p. 291). The following are brief summaries of instructional strategies that Willig and Ortiz (1991) have presented.

Whole Language Approach to Literacy
Teaches writing, language arts and reading through activities which are purposeful, rich in context, build on experiences, student-controlled, grounded in reciprocal interaction. (pp. 291–292)

The Dialogue Journal
Approach in which students are required to write on a regular basis on the topic of their choice. The writer is encouraged to focus on meaning and the communication of ideas, not surface forms of language. The student entries are responded to by the teacher in the journal. Teacher questions and comments on student's topic, without correction, but provides modeling in the response. (pp 292–293)

Fernald's Contextual Approach
This approach integrates reading, spelling, and writing, specifically targets students with reading and learning problems. Students are encouraged to write on self-selected

topics and this writing is used as reading material in initial reading instruction. (p. 293)

Language Experience
Reading instruction that encompasses language arts, writing, listening, and speaking. Learning in context is emphasized. Material to be used for reading is dictated to the teacher by the students after they have experienced a teacher-structured situation. The dictation is used as reading material. (pp. 294–295)

Cooperative Learning Groups
A variety of classroom techniques in which students work on learning activities in small groups of 4 or 5 members, in a structure that encourages mutual cooperation. The focus is primarily on the acquisition of basic skills. Each team is responsible for the learning of all its members and rewards are earned by teams, rather than individuals. (pp. 296–297)

A comprehensive list of competencies for educators of CLDE students follows (see Figure 4). It is taken from Ortiz, Yates, and Garcia (1990). This long list reflects needed training for special educators, classroom instructors, and paraprofessionals involved as service providers.

FIGURE 4
Program Competencies Associated with Serving Language Minority Students

Language Skills*

1. Ability to understand the primary language (L1) spoken by parents and children.
2. Ability to speak L1 and English (L2) fluently in both formal and informal settings.
3. Ability to read and comprehend fully L1 and L2 writing including textbooks, professional journals, and other published works.
4. Ability to write in L1 and L2 with levels of proficiency required for informal as well as professional written communications.
5. Ability to translate instructions, letters and so forth to parents and community members.

Linguistics

1. Understanding of basic concepts regarding the nature of language.
2. Understanding of theories of first and second language acquisition.
3. Ability to identify structural differences between the student's first and second languages, recognizing areas of potential influence and positive transfer.
4. Ability to identify and understand regional, social and developmental varieties in the student's language. (L2 only for ESL)
5. Ability to analyze the child's languages at the phonological, syntactical, morphological, semantic and pragmatic levels. (L2 only for ESL)

Cultural Foundations

1. Understanding of culture in relation to: child-rearing practices, socialization systems and socio-cultural differences in attitudes toward educational attainment, gratification patterns, motivational orientations.
2. Awareness of cross-cultural patterns, practices or attitudes, and their effect on cognitive, affective, behavioral, and motivational development.
3. Understanding of diversity in behavior and learning styles in cross-cultural settings.
4. Understanding of historical origins of local communities.
5. Ability to incorporate contributions of diverse cultural groups into educational programming.

Educational Foundations

1. Knowledge and understanding of the philosophies of general education, bilingual education, special education, bilingual special education, and ESL.
2. Knowledge and understanding of the content of special education, ESL, bilingual education and related areas including handicapping conditions, identification of non- or limited- English proficient students, legislation, litigation, funding, and current research relative to ethnic/linguistic minorities.
3. Ability to apply educational theory and research to instructional programming for handicapped LEP students.
4. Ability to articulate a rationale for bilingual special education and for use of ESL strategies in special education.

Assessment

1. Ability to define the purpose and functions of assessment.
2. Ability to record and utilize observational data.

* Skills for bilingual special educators only.

FIGURE 4 - Continued

3. Knowledge of existing assessment procedures and instruments, both formal and informal, in areas such as: language proficiency, language dominance, language development, cognitive/ intellectual development, perceptual-motor development, social-emotional behavior, adaptive behavior, achievement.
4. Ability to distinguish differences due to socio-cultural background and/or second language learning from handicapping conditions.
5. Ability to recognize potential linguistic and cultural biases of formal and informal assessments and to adapt the evaluation procedure to compensate for such limitations.
6. Ability to select assessment strategies appropriate for ethnic/linguistic minority groups.
7. Ability to test in L1 and L2, and to interpret results including implications for instruction.* (L2 only for ESL)

Instructional Planning

1. Utilization of assessment and other relevant data to plan instructional programs appropriate for bilingual, non-English and limited-English proficient handicapped students.
2. Ability to determine instructional goals based on the identified needs of bilingual, non-English and limited English proficient handicapped students.
3. Ability to write instructional objectives that specify short-term and long-range outcomes for handicapped LEP children.
4. Ability to specify instructional sequences, appropriate teaching/ learning activities, materials, and evaluative procedures specific to the needs of handicapped LEP students.
5. Ability to monitor the effectiveness of instructional sequences, teaching/ learning activities or materials as necessary.
6. Ability to evaluate the effectiveness of instructional strategies and arrangement, and to modify them to meet the unique linguistic and academic needs of exceptional LEP students.
7. Ability to use paraprofessionals effectively.

Instruction

1. Ability to implement varied teaching techniques appropriate for LEP and bilingual students (e.g., mediated learning, the natural language approach, holistic approaches to literacy development, etc.)
2. Ability to manage classroom behavior through application of knowledge related to teaching/learning styles and child-rearing practices.
3. Ability to provide a classroom climate that fosters successful experiences for each student.
4. Ability to provide instruction in L1 and L2 in all curriculum areas of regular and special education.* (L2 only for ESL)
5. Ability to deliver instruction using ESL approaches.

Curriculum

1. Knowledge of program curricula in regular education, special education, bilingual education, ESL and bilingual special education.
2. Ability to adapt or develop curricula to meet the needs of handicapped LEP students.

* Skills for bilingual special educators only.

FIGURE 4 - Continued

3. Ability to edit and revise activities to make them more linguistically and culturally appropriate for handicapped LEP students.
4. Ability to design materials and activities to meet the needs of handicapped LEP students.

Materials

1. Knowledge of sources for materials appropriate for LEP students.
2. Ability to evaluate learning materials in terms of the quality, availability, cost effectiveness, and appropriateness for handicapped LEP students.
3. Ability to secure or produce learning materials that stimulate active, meaningful, purposeful involvement of students in attaining specific learning objectives.

Monitoring/Evaluation

1. Knowledge of program evaluation systems.
2. Ability to design and implement formative and summative evaluation relative to educational interventions and programming for handicapped LEP students.
3. Ability to monitor and adapt individualized instruction.

Counseling

1. Knowledge of the basic theories and/or models in human development and learning specifically related to educating culturally/linguistically diverse groups.
2. Knowledge of: behavior modification with culturally relevant reinforcers, holistic approaches, transactional communicational skills.
3. Ability to serve as a consultant to mainstream personnel who serve LEP handicapped students.

School-Community Relations

1. Ability to effect communication between regular, bilingual, ESL and special education personnel, parents, guardians, child advocates or other personnel involved in the handicapped LEP student's educational program.
2. Ability to work effectively as a member of interdisciplinary teams responsible for the design and implementation of the handicapped LEP student's instructional program.
3. Ability to plan and provide for the direct participation of parents and families of exceptional LEP students in the instructional program and related activities.
4. Knowledge of local community resources for handicapped students.
5. Ability to communicate effectively with parents concerning needs of their handicapped children.

Other

1. Ability to use translators and interpreters effectively.

* Skills for bilingual special educators only.

Note. From Competencies Associated with Serving Exceptional Language Minority Students by A. Ortiz, J. Yates, and S. Garcia, Spring 1990, *The Bilingual Special Education Perspective*, 9, pp. 3–4.
Bilingual Special Education Training Programs, Department of Special Education, The University of Texas at Austin

References

Ambert, A., & Dew, N. *Special education for exceptional bilingual students: A handbook for educators*. Milwaukee: University of Wisconsin, Milwaukee, Midwest National Origin Desegregation Assistance Center.

Baca, L. (1990, September). *Theory and practice in bilingual/cross-cultural special education: Major issues and implications for research, practice, and policy*. Washington, DC: U.S. Government Printing Office.

Baca, L., & Bransford, J. (1982). *An appropriate education for handicapped children of limited English proficiency*. Reston, VA: The Council for Exceptional Children. (ERIC Document Reproduction Service No. 224 265)

Baca, L., & Cervantes, H. (1989). *The bilingual special education interfac*. Columbus, OH: Merrill.

Baca, L., Collier, C., Jacobs, C., & Hill, R. (1991). *Bilingual special education teacher training module: Prereferral intervention*. Boulder, CO: BUENO Center for Multicultural Education, University of Colorado at Boulder.

Bernal, E. (1974). A dialogue on cultural implications for learning. *Exceptional Children, 40*, 552.

Bernstein, D. (1989). Assessing children with limited English proficiency. *Topics in Language Disorders, 9*(3), 15–20.

Blanco, G. (1977). *Bilingual education: Current perspectives*. Arlington, VA: Center for Applied Linguistics.

Bransford, J. & Baca, L. (1989). Bilingual special education: Issues in policy development and implementation. In L. M. Baca & H. T. Cervantes (Eds.), *The bilingual special education interface* (pp. 327–357). Columbus, OH: Merrill.

Brigance, A. H. (1983). Brigance Diagnostic Assessment of Basic Skills (Spanish ed.). Giulio Massano, Ed. Cambridge, MA: Curriculum Associates.

Budoff, M., Gimon, A., & Corman, L. (1974). Learning potential measurement with Spanish-speaking youth as an alternative to IQ tests: A first report. *Interamerican Journal of Psychology, 8*, 233–246.

Calderon, M. (1989, September). Cooperative learning for LEP students. *Intercultural Development Research Association Newsletter, 16*(9), 1–7.

Campione, J. Brown, A., & Ferrara, R. (1982). Mental retardation and intelligence. In R. Sternberg (Ed.), *Handbook of human intelligence* (pp. 392–490). New York: Cambridge University Press.

Carrasquillo, A. L. (1991). Teaching the bilingual special education student. In A. L. Carrasquillo & R. E. Baecher (Eds.), *Bilingual special education: The important connection* (pp. 4–24). Norwood, NJ: Ablex.

Chalfant, J., & Pysh, M. (1981). Teacher assistance teams—A model for within-building problem solving. *Counterpoint,* 16–21.

Chalfant, J., Pysh, M., & Moultrie, R. (1979). Teacher assistance teams: A model for within building problem solving. *Learning Disability Quarterly, 2*(3), 85–96.

Cheng, L. L. (1989). Service delivery to Asian/Pacific LEP children: A cross-cultural framework. *Topics in Language Disorders, 9*(3), 1–14.

Cloud, N. (1988, December). ESL in special education. (ERIC Digest No. ED 303 044)

Cummins, J. (1984). *Bilingualism and special education: Issues in assessment and pedagogy.* San Diego: College-Hill.

Cummins, J. (1986, February). Empowering minority students: A framework for intervention. *Harvard Educational Review, 56*(1), 18–36.

Cummins, J. (1989). A theoretical framework for bilingual special education. *Exceptional Children, 56,* 111–120.

Damico, J. (1991). Descriptive assessment of communicative ability in limited English proficient students. In E. V. Hamayan & J. S. Damico (Eds.), *Limiting bias in the assessment of bilingual students* (pp. 157–218). Austin, TX: Pro-Ed.

Damico, J. S., & Hamayan, E. V. (1991). Implementing assessment in the real world. In E. V. Hamayan & J. S. Damico (Eds.), *Limiting bias in the assessment of bilingual students* (pp. 303–316). Austin, TX: Pro-Ed.

Duran, R. (1988). Testing of linguistic minorities. In R. Linn (Ed.), *Educational measurement* (3rd ed., pp. 573–587). New York: MacMillan.

Duran, R. (1989). Assessment and instruction of at-risk Hispanic students. *Exceptional Children, 56,* 154–159.

Evans, J. (1980, December). *Model pre-school program for handicapped bilingual children.* Austin, TX: Southwest Educational Development Laboratory.

Feuerstein, R. (1979). *The dynamic assessment of retarded performers: The learning potential assessment device. Theory, instruments and techniques.* Baltimore: University Park Press.

Figueroa, R. (1988). *Innovative Approaches Research Project technical proposal.* Davis: University of California.

Figueroa, R. (1989). Psychological testing of linguistic-minority students: Knowledge gaps and regulations. *Exceptional Children, 56,* 145–153.

Figueroa, R., Fradd, S., & Correa, V. (1989). Bilingual special education and this special issue. *Exceptional Children, 56,* 174–178.

Fradd. S. (1987). The changing focus of bilingual education: A guide for administrators. In S. Fradd & W. Tikunoff (Eds.), *Bilingual education and bilingual special education* (pp. 1–44). San Diego: College-Hill.

Fradd, S., & Correa, V. (1989). Meeting the multicultural needs of Hispanic students in special education. *Exceptional Children, 45,* 105–110.

Fradd, S., & Vega, J. (1987). Legal considerations. In S. Fradd & W. Tikunoff (Eds.), *Bilingual and bilingual special education: A guide for administrators* (pp. 45–74). Boston: Little, Brown.

Garcia, S. B., & Ortiz, A. A. (1988). Preventing inappropriate referrals of language miniority students to special education. *New Focus 5,* 1–11.

Gersten, R., & Woodward, J. (1990). The language minority student and special education: A multi-faceted study. *(OSEP Report No. CFDA 84-023H).* Eugene, OR: Eugene Research Institute.

Goldman, S., & Rueda, R. (1988). Developing writing skills in bilingual exceptional children. *Exceptional Children, 54,* 543–551.

Graden, J. (1989). Redefining "preferral" intervention as intervention assistance: collaboration between general and special education. *Exceptional Children, 56,* 227–231.

Hamayan, E. V. (1990, October). *The mainstreaming of LEP students.* Paper presented at the First National Research Symposium on Limited English Proficient Students' Issues, Washington, DC.

Hamayan, E. V., & Damico, J. S. (1991). Developing and using a second language. In E. V. Hamayan & J. C. Damico (Eds.), *Limiting bias in the assessment of bilingual students* (pp. 39–75). Austin, TX: Pro-Ed.

Harris, K., Rueda, R., & Supancheck, P. (1990). A descriptive study of literacy events in secondary special education programs in linguistically diverse schools. *Remedial and Special Education, 2*(4), 20–28.

Hornby, P. (1977). *Bilingualism: Pyschological, social, and educational implications.* New York: Academic Press.

Itard, J.-M.-C. (1962). *The wild boy of Aveyron* (G. Humphrey & M. Humphrey, trans.). Englewood Cliffs, NJ: Prentice-Hall.

Krashen, S. (1982). Providing input for acquisition. In *Principles and practice in second language acquisition* (pp. 58–73). Oxford: Pergamon.

Langdon, H. (1989). Language disorder of difference? Assessing the language skills of Hispanic students. *Exceptional Children, 56,* 160–167.

Lee, A. (1989). A socio-cultural framework for the assessment of Chinese children with special needs, *Topics in Language Disorders, 9*(3), 38–44.

Leon, R. (1991, Spring). Mathematics for culturally and linguistically diverse exceptional children. *La Carta Newsletter of the Bilingual Special Education Program*, pp. 3–5.

Lesser, S. D. (1975). *Improving bilingual instruction and services in special schools*. Brooklyn: New York City Board of Education, Office of Educational Evaluation.

Malherbe, E. (1969). Commentary to N. M. Jones, How and when do persons become bilingual. In L. Kelley (Ed.), *Description and measurement of bilingualism* (p. 78). Toronto: University of Toronto Press.

Mattes, L. J., & Omark, D. R. (1984). *Speech and language assessment for the bilingual handicapped*. San Diego: College-Hill.

McConnell, B. B. (1981, September). *Individualized bilingual instruction: A validated program model effective with bilingual handicapped children*. Paper presented at The Council for Exceptional Children Conference on the Exceptional Bilingual Child, New Orleans.

McLaughlin, B. (Ed.). (1984). *Second language acquisition in childhood: Volume 1*. Hillsdale, NJ: Erlbaum.

Mehen, H. Hertweck, A., Meihls, J. L. (1986). *Handicapping the handicapped: Decision making in students' educational careers*. Palo Alto: Stanford University Press.

Mercer, J. R. (1979). *The system of multicultural pluralistic assessment*. New York: Psychological Corporation.

Mercer, J. R. (1986). *Assessment issues in special education*. Paper presented at the Bilingual Special Education Conference. Pomona: California Polytechnic Institute.

Mercer, J. R., & Rueda, R. (1991, November). *The impact of changing paradigms of disabilities on assessment for special education*. Paper presented at The Council for Exceptional Children Topical Conference on At-Risk Children and Youth, New Orleans.

Moll, L. (1989). Teaching second language students: A Vygotskian perspective. In D. Roen & D. Johnson (Eds.). *Richness in writing: Empowering ESL students* (pp. 55–69). New York: Longman.

Mowder, B. (1980). Strategy for the assessment of bilingual handicapped children. *Psychology in the schools, 17*(1), 7–11.

Oakland, T., & Matuzek, P. (1977). Using tests in nondiscriminatory assessment. In T. Oakland (Ed.), *Psychological and educational assessment of minority children* (pp. 52–69). New York: Brunner/Mazel.

Oller, J., Jr. (1983). Testing proficiencies and diagnosing language disorders in bilingual children. In D. Omark & J. Erickson (Ed.), *The bilingual exceptional child* (pp. 69–88). San Diego: College-Hill.

Ortiz, A. A. (Ed.). (1990a). AIM for the BESt: Update, *The Bilingual Special Education Perspective. 9*, 6–7.

Ortiz, A. A. (1990b). Using school-based problem-solving teams for prereferral intervention. *The Bilingual Special Education Perspective, 10*, 1–5.

Ortiz, A., & Garcia, S. (1988). A prereferral process for preventing inappropriate referrals of Hispanic students to special education. In A. Ortiz & B. Ramirez (Eds.), *Schools and the culturally diverse exceptional student: Promising practices and future directions* (pp. 6–18). Reston, VA: The Council for Exceptional Children.

Ortiz, A., & Maldonado-Colon, E. (1986). Recognizing learning disabilities in bilingual children: How to lessen inappropriate referrals of language minority students to special education. *Journal of Reading, Writing, and Learning Disabilities, 2*(1), 43–56.

Ortiz, A. A., & Yates, J. R. (1983). Incidence among Hispanic exceptionals: Implications for manpower planning. *Journal of the National Association for Bilingual Education, 7*(3), 41–53.

Ortiz, A. A., Yates, J. R., & Garcia, S. B. (1990). Competencies associated with serving exceptional language minority students. *The Bilingual Special Education Perspective, 9*, 1–5.

Plata, M. (1982). *Assessment, placement, and programming of bilingual exceptional pupils: A practical approach.* Reston, VA: The Council for Exceptional Children.

Project Build. (1980). *Bilingual understanding incorporates learning disabilities.* (Final evaluation report, ESEA Title VII Basic Bilingual Education Project, Community School District 4, New York).

Pugach, C., & Johnson, L. (1989). Prereferral interventions: Progress, problems, and challenges. *Exceptional Children, 56*, 217–226.

Richard-Amato, P. A. (Ed.). (1988). *Making it happen: Interaction in the second language classroom.* New York: Longman.

Rivera, C. (1990). *Project, purposes, and approaches.* Washington, DC: U.S. Department of Education, Office of Bilingual and Minority Language Affairs.

Rueda, R. (1984). Metalinguistic awareness in monolingual and bilingual mildly retarded children. *Journal of the National Association for Bilingual Education, 8*, 55–67.

Rueda, R. (1988). Defining mild disabilities with language-minority students. *Exceptional Children, 56*, 121–129.

Rueda, R., & Chan, K. (1979). Poverty and culture in special education: Separate but equal. *Exceptional Children, 45*, 422–431.

Ruiz, N. (1988). *Implementing effective practices: A guide for teachers of Hispanic learning handicapped students.* Unpublished manuscript, University of California at Davis Linguistic Minorities Research Project.

Ruiz, N. (1989). An optimal learning environment for Rosemary. *Exceptional Children, 56,* 130–144.

Samora-Curry, S. (1990, Spring). *Alternative method for assessing language.* Paper presented at University College at Buffalo Colloquium: Content Area Bilingual Education.

Vasquez Nuttall, E., Goldman, P., & Landurand, P. (1983). A study of mainstreamed limited English proficient handicapped students in bilingual education. Newton, MA: Vasquez Nuttall Associates.

Weiss, R. (1980). *Efficacy and cost effectiveness of an early intervention program for young handicapped children.* Paper presented at the Handicapped Children's Early Education Program (HCEEP) project director's meeting, Washington, DC.

Whitaker, J., & Prieto, A. (1989). The effects of cultural and linguistic variables on the academic achievement of minority children. *Focus on Exceptional Children, 21*(5), 1–10.

Wilde, J. B. (Ed.). (1991). Test Briefs: Testing the special education bilingual student. *EAC-West News, 4*(3), 4.

Willig, A. C., & Ortiz, A. A. (1991). The nonbiased individualized education program: Linking assessment to instruction. In E. V. Hamayan & J. S. Damico (Eds.), *Limiting bias in the assessment of bilingual students* (pp. 281–302). Austin, TX: Pro-Ed.

Resources

Federal Agencies

Office of Bilingual Education and Minority Languages Affairs (OBEMLA)
U.S. Department of Education
400 Maryland Ave. S. W.
Washington, DC 20202
(202) 732-5063
FAX (202) 732-5737

Office of Special Education and Rehabilitation Services (OSERS)
U.S. Department of Education
400 Maryland Ave. S. W.
Washington, DC 20202
(202) 732-1265

Research and Development Center

The National Center for Research on Cultural Diversity and Second Language Learning
399 Clark Kerr Hall
Eugene Garcia, Barry McLaughlin, Co-Directors
University of California at Santa Cruz
Santa Cruz, CA 95064
(408) 459-3500
FAX (408) 459-3502

OBEMLA Bilingual Special Education Resource Center

FAU Multifunctional Resource Center
Ann Willig, Director
Florida Atlantic University
College of Education
500 Northwest 20th Street-MT 17
Boca Raton, FL 33431
(407) 367-2301
FAX (407) 367-3759

Dissemination Organizations

The Council for Exceptional Children (CEC)
1920 Association Drive
Reston, VA 22091-1589
(703) 620-3660
FAX (703) 264-9494

Bilingual Special Education Program
Department of Special Education
Education Building 306
The University of Texas at Austin
Austin, TX 78712-1290
(512) 471-6244

ERIC Clearinghouse on
Elementary and Early Childhood
University of Illinois
College of Education
805 West Pennsylvania Avenue
Urbana, IL 61801-4897
(217) 333-1386

ERIC Clearinghouse on
Handicapped and Gifted Children
The Council for Exceptional
Children
1920 Association Drive
Reston, VA 22091-1589
(703) 620-3660
FAX (703) 264-9494

ERIC Clearinghouse on Languages
and Linguistics
Center for Applied Linguistics
1118 22nd Street, N.W.
Washington, DC 20037
(202) 429-9292
FAX (202) 659-5641

Federal Reegional Resource Center
(Special Education)
University of Kentucky
314 Mineral Industries Building
Lexington, KY 40506-0051
(606) 257-1337

National Clearinghouse for
Bilingual Education (NCBE)
1118 22nd Street, N. W.
Washington, DC 20037
(202) 467-0867 1-800-321-NCBE
FAX (202) 429-9766

National Clearinghouse on Women
and Girls with Disabilities
C/O Educational Equity
Concepts
Ellen Rubin
114 East 32 Street
New York, NY 10016
(212) 725-1803
A national, nonprofit
organization to eliminate bias
due to sex, race, and disability
(see Training Modules/Material
section).

National Information Center for
Children and Youth with
Handicaps (NICHY)
P. O. Box 1492
Washington, DC 20013
1-800-999-5599 (toll free)

Resources in Special Education
(RiSE)
650 Howe Avenue Suite 300
Sacramento, CA 95825
(916) 641-5925
FAX (916) 641-5871

Special Issues

American Speech and Hearing Association (ASHA)
September 1989; Volume 31
"Multicultural Populations"
2600 South First Street
Springfield, IL 62717
(301) 897-5700 1-800-638-8255

American Speech and Hearing Association ASHA
June 1985; Volume 27 No. 6
"Minority Concerns: A Major Issue"
2600 South First Street
Springfield, IL 62717
(301) 897-5700 1-800-638-8255

Annotated Bibliography of Research and Professional Publications Relevant to the Education of Handicapped, Limited English Proficient Students and Their Families
September 1990
Sandra H. Fradd, Ph.D.
Disseminated by the National Clearinghouse for Bilingual Education (NCBE)
1118 22nd Street, N.W.
Washington, DC 20037
(202) 467-0867 1-800-321-NCBE
FAX (202) 429-9766

Exceptional Children
October 1989; Volume 56, Number 2
"Meeting the Multicultural Needs of the Hispanic Students in Special Education"
The Council for Exceptional Children
1920 Association Drive
Reston, VA 22091-1589
(703) 620-3660
FAX (703) 264-9494

Flyer File: Culturally and Linguistically Different Exceptional Learners
A product of the ERIC Clearinghouse on Handicapped and Gifted Children
The Council for Exceptional Children
1920 Association Drive
Reston, VA 22091-1589
(703) 620-3660
FAX (703) 264-9494

The Journal of Educational Issues of Language Minority Students
Summer 1990; Volume 7
Boise State University, Boise
The Bilingual Education Teacher Preparation Program
1910 University Drive
Education Building 215
Boise, ID 83725
(208) 385-1194

Office of Special Education and Rehabilitation Services OSERS News in Print
Spring 1991; Volume 3, Number 4
"Disability and People from Minority Backgrounds"
United States Department of Education
Room 3129, Switzer Building
330 C. Street S.W.
Washington, DC 20202-2524
(202) 732-1723

Resources in Special Education RiSE
1989; Volume 4, Number 3
"The Special EDge"
650 Howe Avenue Suite 300
Sacramento, CA 95825
(916) 641-5925
FAX (916) 641-5871

Sensitive to the Educational Needs of Growing Americans (SENGA)
Summer 1989; Volume 1, Number 1
"Issues That Should be Considered in the Assessment of Black Children"
P. O. Box 26818
New Orleans, LA 70186-6818
(504) 242-6022

Sensitive to the Educational Needs of Growing Americans (SENGA)
Fall 1991 Volume 1, Number 3
"Special Issue: Celebrate Diversity"
P. O. Box 26818
New Orleans, LA 70186-6818
(504) 242-6022

Teacher Education and Special Education
Winter 1991; Volume 14, Number 1
"Diverse Exceptional Learners"
The Council for Exceptional Children
Teacher Education Division
Special Press
474 North Lakeshore Drive, Suite 3910
Chicago, IL 60611
(312) 464-3374

Newsletters

The Bilingual Special Education Perspective
The University of Texas at Austin
College of Education
Department of Special Education EDB 306
Austin, TX 78712-1290
(512) 471-6244

Buenos Dias
BUENO Center for Multicultural Education, School of Ed
Room 255 Campus Box 249
University of Colorado
Boulder, CO 80309-0249
(303) 492-5416

CEC Ethnic and Multicultural Bulletin
The Council for Exceptional Children
1920 Associate Drive
Reston, VA 22091-1589
(703) 620-3660 FAX (703) 264-9494

Division for Culturally and Linguistically Diverse Exceptional Learners (DDEL)
The Council for Exceptional Children
1920 Association Drive
Reston, VA 22091-1589
(703) 620-3660
FAX (703) 264-9494

EAC-WEST News
Evaluation Assistance Center, Western Region
The University of New Mexico
College of Education
EAC-West
Albuquerque, NM 87131
(505) 277-7281 (800) 247-4269

LA CARTA Newsletter of the Bilingual Special Education Program
Exceptional Special Education Program
State University College at Buffalo
1300 Elmwood Avenue
Buffalo, NY 14222
(716) 878-3038

Training Modules/Materials

BUENO Bilingual Special Education Modules
August 1991
BUENO Center for Multicultural Education
Education Building Campus Box 249
University of Colorado
Boulder, CO 80303
(303) 492-5416
Staff development training modules focusing on CLDE students.

Bilingual/ESOL Special Education Collaboration and Reform Project
1990
Project Director: Sandra H. Fradd Ph. D.
University of Miami
222 Merrick Building
Coral Gables, FL 33124
(904) 392-2046

Interpreter/Translator in the School Setting Module
Spring 1988
Resources in Special Education (RISE)
650 Howe Avenue Suite 300
Sacramento, CA 95825
(916) 641-5925 FAX (916) 641-5871

Mainstreaming for Equity
Resource and Activity Kits
Kit 1 (K–2) Focus on Family and
School: Teaching about Hearing
and Mobility. Kit 2 (3–6) The
Communication Kit: Teaching
About Visual and Hearing
Impairment.
National Clearinghouse on
Women and Girls with
Disabilities
C/O Educational Equity
Concepts
Ellen Rubin
114 East 32nd Street
New York, NY 10016
(212) 725-1803

Multisystem Systematic
Instructional Planning for
Exceptional Bilingual Students
1989.
The Council for Exceptional
Children
1920 Association Drive
Reston, VA 22091-1589
(703) 620-3660
FAX (703) 264-9494

Directory of Persons

Higher Education
Representatives

Leonard Baca
Professor, Bilingual Special
Education
BUENO Center for
Multicultural Education
Education Building
University of Colorado
Campus Box 249
Boulder, CO 80309
(303) 492-5416

Li-Rong Lilly Cheng
Health & Human Services
San Diego State University
San Diego, CA 92182-0409
(619) 594-6898

Philip Chinn
Division of Special Education
California State University-
Los Angeles
5151 State University Drive
Los Angeles, CA 90032
(213) 343-4409

Nancy Cloud
Assistant Professor, Special
Education
208 Mason Hall
Hofstra University
Hempstead, NY 11550
(516) 463-5769

Catherine Collier
Assistant to the Vice President
Portland State University
P. O. Box 751
Portland, OR 97207-0751
(503) 725-4422

Jim Cummins
Ontario Institute for the Study
of Education
Modern Language Center
University of Ottawa
252 Bloor Street
Toronto, Ontario, Canada
M5SLV6
(416) 923-6441

Sarita Samora Curry
Associate Professor
Buffalo State College
1300 Elmwood Avenue
Buffalo, NY 14222
(716) 878-5309

Jack S. Damico
University of Southwestern
Louisiana
Department of Communicative
Disorders
P.O. Box 43170
Lafayette, LA 70504
(318) 231-6721

Elva Duran
Associate Professor, Special
Education
California State University,
Sacramento
School of Education
Department of Special
Education, Rehabilitation, &
School Psychology
Sacramento, CA 95819-2694
(916) 278-6622

Norma Ewing
Department Chairperson
Department of Special Education
Pulliam Hall, Room 129
Southern Illinois University
Carbondale, IL 62901
(618)453-2524 or 253-2311

Richard Figueroa
University of California, Davis
Department of Education
Kerr Hall
Davis, CA 95616
(916) 752-6293

Sandra Fradd
University of Miami
222 Merrick Building
Coral Gables, FL
(904) 392-2046

Robert Gallegos
2348 Terrace Court
Las Cruces, NM 88001
(505) 646-1941

Ann Gallegos
2348 Terrace Court
Las Cruces, NM 88001
(505) 646-1941

Shernaz Garcia
Lecturer and Program
Coordinator
Bilingual Special Education
The University of Texas at
Austin
EDB 306
Austin, TX 78512-1290
(512) 471-6244

Russell Gersten
Eugene Research Institute
1400 High Street, Suite C
Eugene, OR 97401
(503) 342-1553

Herb Grossman, Professor
School of Education
San Jose State University
San Jose, CA 95192
(408) 924-3692

Kathy Harris
Arizona State University West
Education & Human Services
P. O. Box 37100
Phoenix, AZ 85069
(602) 543-6339

Else V. Hamayan
Coordinator of Training and
Services
Illinois Resource Center
2360 East Devon Avenue, Suite
3011
Des Plaines, IL 60018
(312) 296-6070

Norma Iribarren
Florida Atlantic University
Multi-Function Center
M. T. 17 College of Education
500 Northwest 20th Street
Boca Raton, FL 33431
(407) 367-3943

Marilyn Johnson
Director
Northern Arizona University
American Indian Rehabilitation
Research & Training Center
P. O. Box 5630
Flagstaff, AZ 86011
(602) 523-4791

Rosa Leon
Assistant Professor, Department
of Special Education
New York State College at
Buffalo
300 Elmwood Avenue
Buffalo, NY 14222
(716) 878-5309

Esther Leung
Professor
Department of Special Education
Wallace 245
Eastern Kentucky University
Richmond, KY 40475
(606) 622-4442

Elba Maldonado-Colon
Associate Professor
San Jose State University
Division of Special Education
Sweeney Hall 204
870 East El Camino Real
San Jose, CA 95192
(408) 924-3786

Jane Mercer
Professor of Sociology
University of California at
Riverside
Riverside, CA 92521
(714) 787-4343

Isaudra Metz
Department of Special Education
University of New Mexico
Albuquerque, NM
(505) 277-2231

Ofelia Miramontes
BUENO Center for
Multicultural Education
Education Building
University of Colorado
Campus Box 249
Boulder, CO 80309
(303) 492-5416

Mada Kay Morehead
Director of Research and
Planning
Kyrene School District
Tempe, AZ 85287
(602) 496-4682

Alba Ortiz
Professor and Associate Dean of
Academic Affairs and Research
College of Education
University of Texas at Austin
Austin, TX 78712
(512) 471-6244

Alfonso Prieto
Professor, Department of
Special Education
Arizona State University
Tempe, AZ 85287-2011
(602) 965-1458

Robert Rueda
Associate Professor
Department of Curriculum
Teaching and Special Education
University of Southern
California
Los Angeles, CA 90089-0031
(213) 740-3463

Nadine Ruiz
University of California, Davis
Department of Education
Kerr Hall
Davis, CA 95616
(916) 752-6628

Alicia Paredes Scribner
Research Associate and Lecturer
College of Education
University of Texas at Austin
EBD 306
Austin, TX 78735
(512) 471-6244

Jerry Tafoya
National Faculty,
American Psychological
Association
#323 2250 24th Street
San Francisco, CA 94107
(415) 821-9518

Ann C. Willig
Florida Atlantic University
337 Southwest 28th Avenue
Delray Beach, FL 33445
(407) 367-2301

John Woodward
Eugene Research Institute
1400 High Street, Suite C
Eugene, Or 97401
(503) 342-1553

James R. Yates
Professor and Chair
Department of Education
Administration
9600 Gambel's Quail
Austin, TX 78758
(512) 471-7551

Stan Zucker
Professor of Special Education
College of Education
Arizona State University
Tempe, AZ 85287
(602) 965-6156

CEC Mini-Library
Exceptional Children at Risk

A set of 11 books that provide practical strategies and interventions for children at risk.

- *Programming for Aggressive and Violent Students.* Richard L. Simpson, Brenda Smith Miles, Brenda L. Walker, Christina K. Ormsbee, & Joyce Anderson Downing. No. P350. 1991. 42 pages.

- *Abuse and Neglect of Exceptional Children.* Cynthia L. Warger with Stephanna Tewey & Marjorie Megivern. No. P351. 1991. 44 pages.

- *Special Health Care in the School.* Terry Heintz Caldwell, Barbara Sirvis, Ann Witt Todaro, & Debbie S. Accouloumre. No. P352. 1991. 56 pages.

- *Homeless and in Need of Special Education.* L. Juane Heflin & Kathryn Rudy. No. P353. 1991. 46 pages.

- *Hidden Youth: Dropouts from Special Education.* Donald L. Macmillan. No. P354. 1991. 37 pages.

- *Born Substance Exposed, Educationally Vulnerable.* Lisbeth J. Vincent, Marie Kanne Poulsen, Carol K. Cole, Geneva Woodruff, & Dan R. Griffith. No. P355. 1991. 28 pages.

- *Depression and Suicide: Special Education Students at Risk.* Eleanor C. Guetzloe. No. P356. 1991. 45 pages.

- *Language Minority Students with Disabilities.* Leonard M. Baca & Estella Almanza. No P357. 1991. 56 pages.

- *Alcohol and Other Drugs: Use, Abuse, and Disabilities.* Peter E. Leone. No. P358. 1991. 33 pages.

- *Rural, Exceptional, At Risk.* Doris Helge. No. P359. 1991. 48 pages.

- *Double Jeopardy: Pregnant and Parenting Youth in Special Education.* Lynne Muccigrosso, Marylou Scavarda, Ronda Simpson-Brown, & Barbara E. Thalacker. No. P360. 1991. 44 pages.

Save 10% by ordering the entire library, No. P361, 1991. Call for the most current price information, 703/620-3660.

Send orders to:
The Council for Exceptional Children, Dept. K11150
1920 Association Drive, Reston VA 22091-1589